ABOUT THE AUTHOR

David Yeadon is a city planner who tired of big-city life in Los Angeles and set out to explore those hidden parts of California, which too few of us have a chance to see.

Mr. Yeadon, who has spent much of his life in Europe and the Middle East, is fascinated by the tangible and short history of California. During his months of travel through back lanes and tiny villages, he spent much of his time talking to local inhabitants and pouring over time-worn books in dusty libraries in an effort to capsulize the fascinating history of the small, often little-known towns scattered around the southern half of the State.

Small Towns is the result and Mr. Yeadon hopes that his sketches and notes will generate a fresh interest in those parts of California still largely undiscovered by tourists and southland residents alike.

exploring

SMALL TOWNS

1. SOUTHERN CALIFORNIA

david yeadon
the ward ritchie press

FOR MY MOTHER AND FATHER

SAN JOAQUIN VALLEY & SIERRAS
CENTRAL COAST
THE DESERT
LOS ANGELES FRINGE
THE BACK COUNTRY
IMPERIAL VALLEY

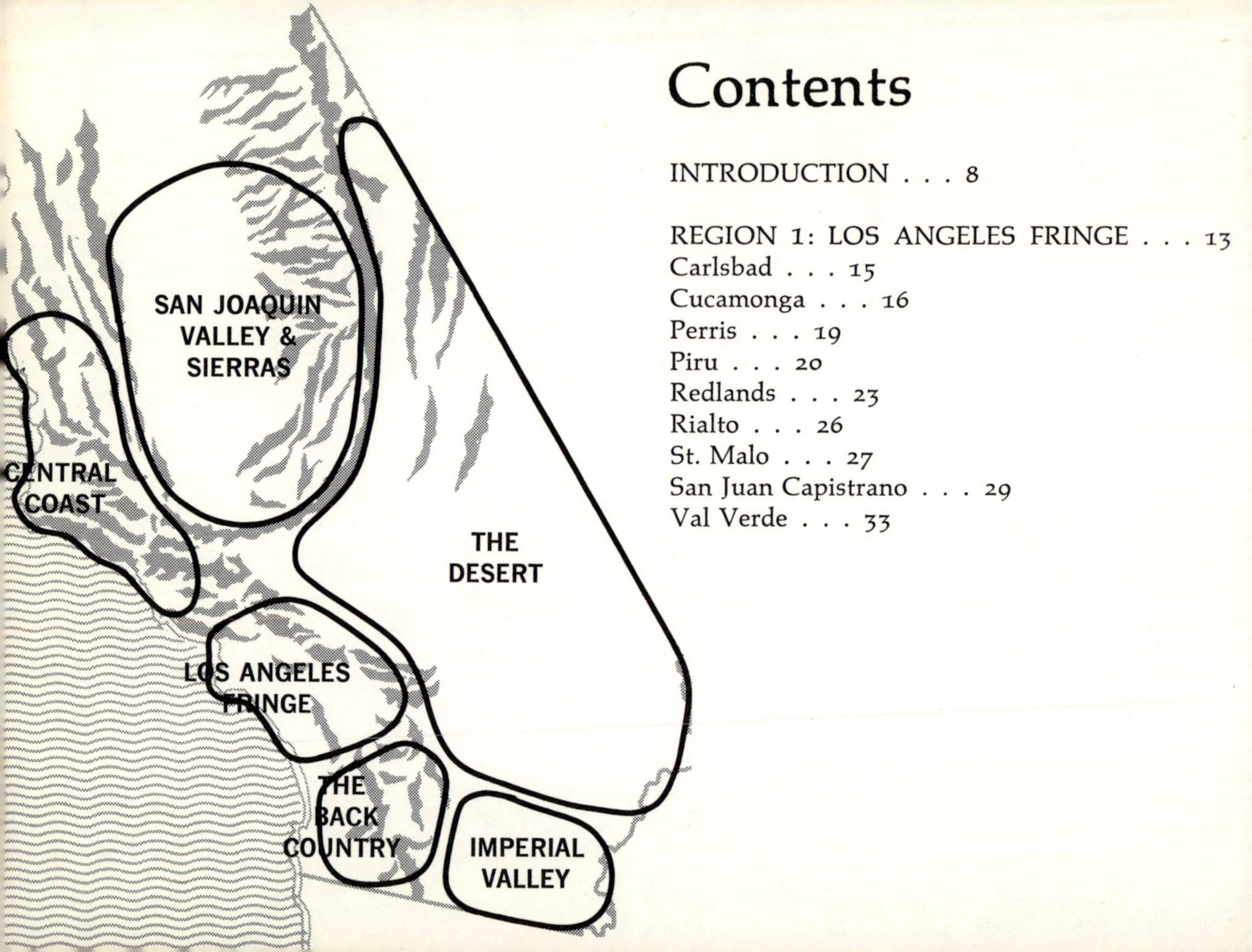

Contents

Introduction

It all started the day I wandered, almost by accident, into the tiny town of Piru. I was on my way to join thousands of other tan-seeking Californians on the beaches north of Ventura and happened to spot a wind-worn, almost illegible hand-painted sign which pointed up a narrow leafy lane and read "Piru—one mile." As it was, I needed something to quake a nagging thirst, so leaving the main road which ran through the Santa Clara Valley, I drove up the tree-covered hillside.

It was like going back to the turn of the century. The old general store sat facing a delicate, slightly lopsided hotel with wide, shaded verandahs and small dark windows. Just down the road an old abandoned railroad station decayed in sombre silence beside the rusty tracks. Brittle autumn leaves had piled up against the station-master's office, almost covering a sign which read "This station will be closed temporarily." It was dated 1937.

High on the hillside above the sleepy town, a great mansion complete with towers, turrets, stained-glass windows and a baronial entrance sat staring arrogantly across the orange orchards in the valley below. The driveway, dusty from lack of use, was lined with overgrown shrubs and the large lawn had not been cut for many months. But somehow the unkempt grounds paled into insignificance against the proud Victorian house. I found out later as I talked with people in the town below that this had been the home of David C. Cook, a deeply religious millionaire from the mid-west who had founded Piru as his own private Garden of Eden, imposing a strict code of ethical behavior on all whom he permitted to live in his paradise.

Sometime later, I discussed this strange little community with colleagues in Los Angeles and was surprised to learn that, without exception, no one had ever heard of, let alone visited, Piru. I began to wonder how many other little-known communities like Piru still existed in southern California. So giving up my usual visits to overcrowded beaches, and the other all-too-familiar centers of gregariousness, I started slowly to explore (sketch book in hand) those lanes and byways, little used by others.

What I found is recorded in this book. Of course it is not intended as an exhaustive tome of local histories. This has already been achieved by authors far better equipped than myself who have been endowed with a level of patience and endurance which I can only regard with envy and awe. Instead, I have assumed on the part of the reader a basic familiarity with the primary aspects of Californian history and have tried merely to extend his appreciation of the western heritage—its richness, variety and fascination.

A town is like a child. It is continually changing in response to external or internal forces yet maintains a semblance, no matter how small, of its original form, character and idiosyncrasies. As the reader works slowly through the book he will be introduced to towns which have moved through many phases of growth during their relatively short existence. He will find towns like Elsinore near the Santa Ana Mountains which began as a small, highly moral and temperate community in 1885, then became a fashionable film star resort complete with Hollywood-influenced architecture, then experienced a period of numbing decline before recapturing its resort and recreation image. Other towns, in fact many of southern California's small towns, began as railroad stops on the trans-continental or inter-State railroads. Some were never more than names on a map; others such as Hanford, Perris, Carlsbad and Redlands grew into substantial communities. The unfortunate Heber, in the Imperial Valley, prepared itself especially for its role as a great metropolis at the junction of two major lines only to find its fine aspirations shattered when the junction was moved northwards to El Centro, today a flourishing city.

Some towns, although retaining fine titles, are in fact virtually non-existent. Date City, in the Imperial Valley, is merely a store, as is Boulevard near the Cleveland Forest. Keysville, high up in the Sierras near Lake Isabella, consists of two shacks and the remains of an earthworks fortification constructed in the 1850's to withstand Indian attacks—which never came! High in the Owens Valley is, or rather was, Manzanar, a rehabilitation town for Japanese during World War II. Today all that can be found there is an oriental-styled gatehouse.

The great gold mining era of 1850-80 brought a rash of instant towns to California, many of which have long since disappeared. However Julian, in the back country around San Diego, Randsburg, and Keeler still exist, and the preserved town of Bodie, way up in the high desert, is one of the most fascinating "ghost" settlements in the State.

Perhaps the most successful small towns today are the resort communities such as Cayucos,

Oceano, and Carlsbad, which still retain their prime assets—the sea and the beach. Other resort communities, particularly those which relied upon hot springs and mineral waters usually found along the earthquake belt are less successful. Jacumba, with its magnificent mission-styled hotel and spa is a sleepy community almost on the Mexican border. While the stucco flakes from unpainted walls, the residents remember the boom-years of the 20's.

The one unfortunate feature that is prevalent throughout many small towns in the State is the lack of concern or interest in the retention of buildings which reflect the richness and quality of the Californian heritage. In Oceano, for example, the magnificently ornate Coffee T. Rice House crumbles at the rear of the mobile home park which occupies what was once its front lawn. In Rialto one of the finest wooden churches in the metropolitan area is disintegrating while local historical societies pass the buck to one another. Even the famous Warner Ranch which has been blessed with the title of "historical monument" is unlikely to last out the decade unless urgent and thorough renovation is undertaken.

Maybe the problem is that California's growth has been so rapid in so brief a period that there has been little time for concern over preservation and retention of a fascinating heritage. However, unless some concerted effort on the part of State and local agencies is forthcoming—and inevitably (albeit unfortunately) this implies financial effort—there will be little left in the future to remind Californians of this heritage beyond a few photographs and books like "Small Towns." Our grandchildren may well wonder what happened to our values.

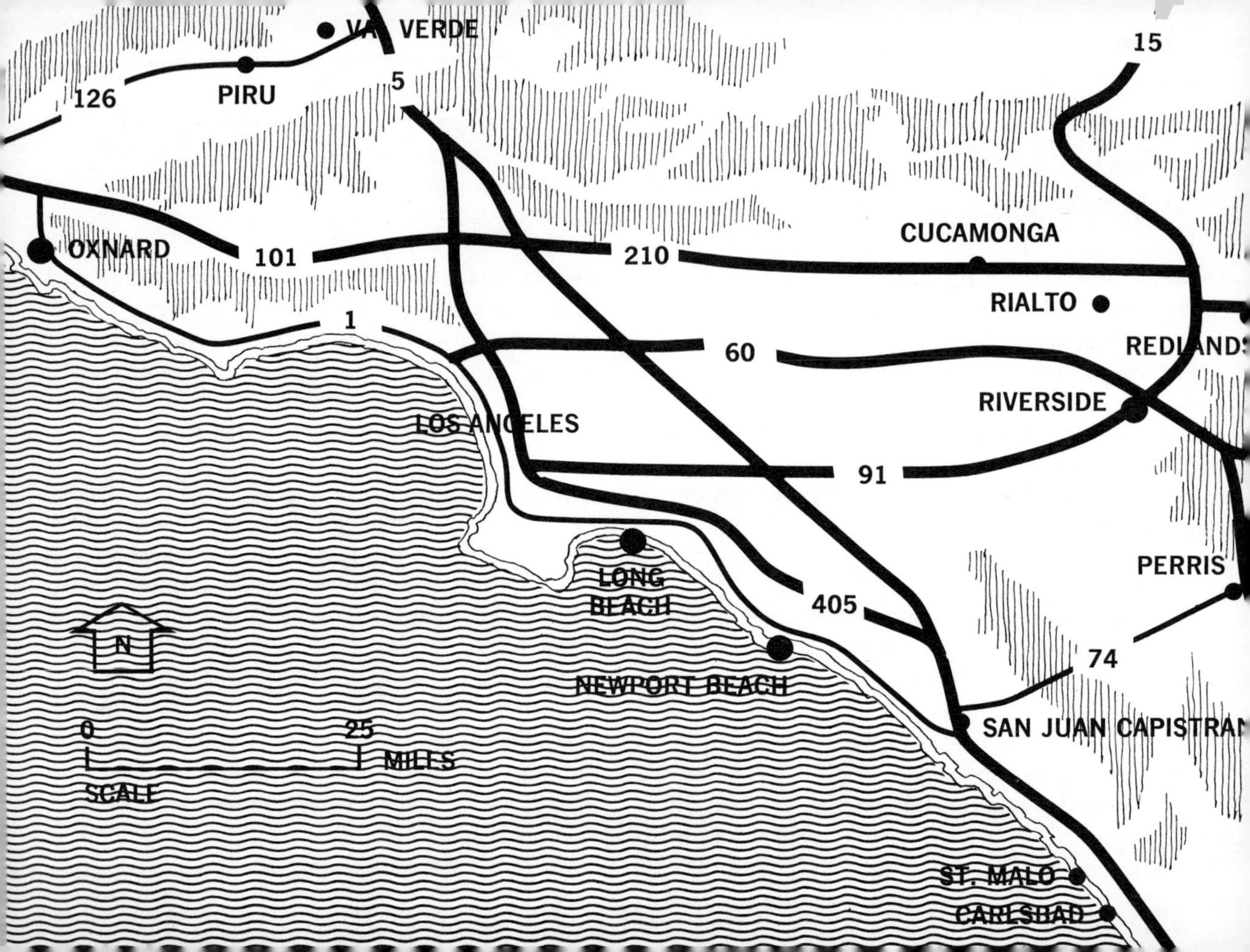
VAL VERDE
PIRU
126
5
15
OXNARD
101
210
CUCAMONGA
RIALTO
REDLANDS
1
60
RIVERSIDE
LOS ANGELES
91
LONG BEACH
PERRIS
405
N
NEWPORT BEACH
74
0
25
MILES
SCALE
SAN JUAN CAPISTRANO
ST. MALO
CARLSBAD

Los Angeles Fringe

This great sprawling metropolitan region, home of more than 8 million people, began in 1781 as a dusty little Spanish pueblo with the resounding name of *El Pueblo de Nuestra Señora La Reina de Los Angeles de Porciuncula*. During its initial years the town's growth was not impressive and by the early 1800's it could only claim a resident population of 300. However, following the Mexican takeover from the Spaniards in 1821 and subsequent secularization of the Mission lands, Los Angeles experienced its first minor boom and in 1835 was granted the title of *ciudad* or city.

However, not until the Low-Sierra goldrush of the late-1850's and the opening up of the Southern Pacific and Santa Fe railroads in the '70's did Los Angeles begin to experience the first major booms which were to make it one of the largest cities in the world. During this period, extensive advertising campaigns which claimed Los Angeles and California as a "veritable 'Garden of Eden'" and boasted "room for millions," attracted tens of thousands of East coast and mid-West residents to this "paradise on earth." Communities such as Redlands sprang up as elite centers for the wealthy, complete with neo-classic railroad stations and palatial mansions dripping with gingerbread and all the "Carpenter-Gothic" trimmings of the Victorian era. Others like Piru reflected the Elysian dreams of individuals.

Los Angeles continued to grow. The discovery of oil, the amazing development of the motion picture industry and the prosperous orchards of the San Fernando Valley were all major dynamic forces which thrust the city outwards. Bunker Hill, a once fashionable residential nucleus for the top strata of society, gave way to more outlying communities. Towns like Carlsbad and St. Malo became exclusive resort centers. The increasing use of the automobile, the abundance of flat land and a paranoid fear of earthquakes and fires (recurring disasters in San Francisco had been carefully noted) produced a "sprawl" of development throughout the basin and valley, unmatched by any other city in the world. Today, to the uninitiated visitor, this is one of Los Angeles' most striking (or alarming) features.

TWIN
INNS

Carlsbad

THE PLACE OF STINKING WATERS

Not a very imposing title for a town—but that's what the Spanish explorer Gaspar de Portola called the area in 1769 when he and his band of soldiers camped adjoining a local swamp and named it Agua Hedionda Lagoon.

Carlsbad itself was not founded until the late 1880's when John Frazer discovered mineral springs, identical in content and quality to those found in Karlsbad, the famous Bohemian Spa. Frazier formed a land company and within a short time the area was booming with eastern settlers attracted by the climate and easy accessibility on newly constructed railroads.

The Twin Inns—now a fine restaurant—is one of the last of the great mansions which graced the town. The delightfully "chic" railroad station is today the home of the local Chamber of Commerce.

OLD RAILROAD STATION • CARLSBAD

THOMAS WINERY · CUCAMONGA

Cucamonga
CALIFORNIA'S OLDEST WINERY

Not only is the Thomas Winery in Cucamonga the oldest in California but claims to be the second oldest in the U.S.A. It all began in 1839 when Tiburcio Tapia was granted the Cucamonga Ranch by Governor Juan Batista of Mexico. Tapia built himself an adobe home and planted his first twelve rows of grapes (which remained in fertile production for almost 100 years).

Today the winery is owned and operated by the Filippi family who long before they emigrated to the U.S.A. in 1922 were famous for their fine wines produced in the north of Italy, near Venice.

Disaster struck this winery in 1969 when a period of unprecedented rainfall over the San Gabriels brought torrential floods which destroyed much of the vineyards and washed away the old adobe homestead. Today everything is back to normal and the main building of the winery with its huge wooden doors and old waterwheel contains a fascinating collection of old photographs and relics in addition, of course, to a wine-tasting bar which seems to be its prime attraction.

WINERY WATERWHEEL · CUCAMONGA

PERRIS
PERRIS

Perris

THE ROCK CASTLE

Looking like an impenetrable castle guarding the entrance to this sleepy agricultural town, the Rock Castle in Perris is the work of the Ragsdale family who used to operate a service station in the town. During 1928 and 1929 the Ragsdales drove their model "T" Ford out into the desert washes around Banning to select, stone by stone, the building materials for their unusual house. Even though the walls of the house are over six feet thick in places, there was a surplus of stones after construction and these now adorn fireplaces and patios throughout the town.

Perris began as a small agricultural community in the 1880's. Ambitious plans for the town's growth resulted in the construction of this delicate railroad station in 1886 on the San Bernardino to San Diego main line. Unfortunately, due mainly to problems of water shortage in the valley, growth was not so rapid as expected. The station was closed and plans are in progress to use it as a museum.

ROCK HOUSE • PERRIS

Piru

PLANS FOR PARADISE

When David C. Cook, a renowned publisher of religious books from Illinois, moved into the Santa Clara Valley in 1886, he had dreams of creating a new garden of Eden on the slopes of the Los Padres Forest. He purchased the 14,000 acre Rancho Temescal, founded a little community complete with hotel and church and began the development of extensive orchards and vineyards in the fertile valley.

He located his own house—an elaborate "gingerbread" mansion—on a knoll overlooking the rest of the town (note the recess carved in the shape of a "C" for Cook just to the left of the turreted tower).

From all accounts Cook was a devoutly spiritual man and demanded vows of abstinence from all his workers. Any evidence of drinking, smoking or foul language could lead to immediate expulsion from this earthly paradise. Unfortunately the influx of wildcat oil prospectors into the area and the growing prosperity of the valley soon began eroding away Cook's little domain. He left, hurt and disillusioned, and never returned.

The house is still in excellent condition and recent additions include an ornate lampost (with ER II—Queen Elizabeth the Second—stamped on the base). Similar lamposts still grace the Thames embankment in London.

COOK MANSION   •   PIRU

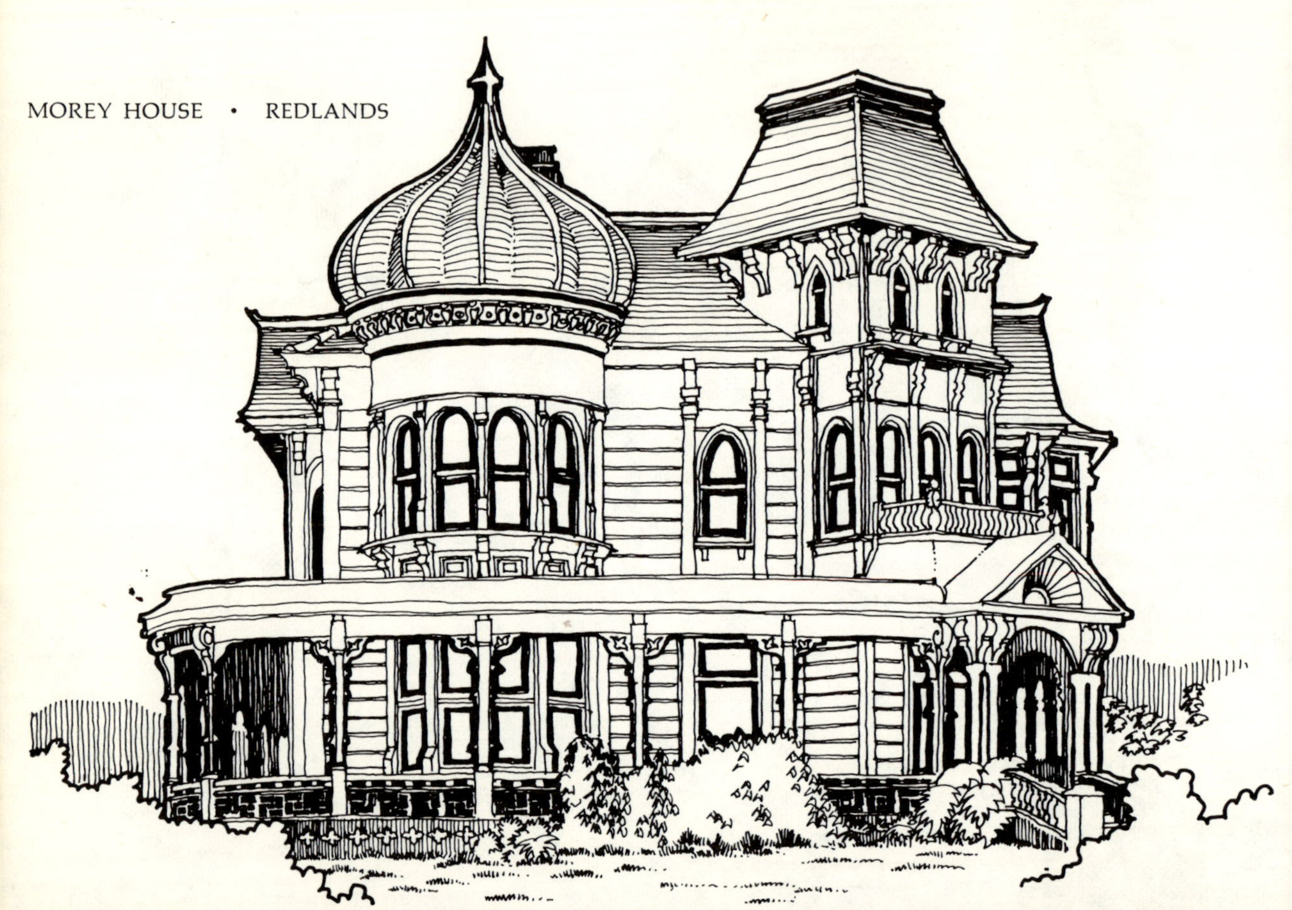

MOREY HOUSE · REDLANDS

Redlands

THE REDLAND VICTORIANS

The dignified city of Redlands sits sedately in a natural amphitheatre at the eastern end of the San Bernardino valley. From its inception in 1881 as a favorite winter resort and retirement center for wealthy east coast and Chicago citizens, Redlands has been lavishly praised by residents and visitors alike. William Devol, in his book *Scenic America* (published 1912), described the city in extravagant Victorian prose as:

"Smiling serenely, contentedly, securely as in the hollow of God's hand."

Few towns can boast a railroad station of this calibre. It was Mayor Homer Kinsbury who, stressing the importance of Redlands as a passenger and freight center, bludgeoned the Santa Fe Company into constructing this classical edifice in 1908. Ironically from that year onward passenger trade diminished in favor of the automobile!

High on the heavily landscaped slopes above the business district can be found one of the finest collections of late Victorian architecture in the country. The Morey House (1882) is almost totally surrounded by lemon groves. The house contains a wild mixture of architectural influences including a mansard roof on the one hand, and an Islamic dome on the other, with a delicate traceried veranda as a strong unifying element.

Further to the east, on Cajon Street, is the mag-

nificent Edwards House (1890) which once sat proudly in twenty acres of garden but today is partially blocked from view by modern single story development which lines the street.

The exotically Spanish styled mansion on Olive Street is one of the most unique homes in this area. Originally built in 1903 for the wealthy capitalist W. H. Holt, the two story stucco structure features a basement which stretches the length of the house and contains a full-sized bowling alley. Harold Bell Wright, the author of that famous Western classic *The Winning of Barbara Worth* lived in the garage apartment while preparing his manuscript.

Every year in early December, the YWCA in Redlands organizes a one day open-house tour of some of the magnificent old Victorian mansions —most of which are still beautifully preserved.

Rialto

THE CHURCH NOBODY WANTED

This extremely rich and well-detailed Wesleyan church today sits in a sad state of disrepair just off Riverside Avenue in Rialto.

It was built in 1906 and dedicated in 1907 by that famous early Californian writer, Harold Bell Wright, who wrote his best known novel *The Winning of Barbara Worth* in nearby Redlands.

Due to increasing costs of maintenance and a diminishing congregation attendance, its use as a church declined. Inevitably vandals began to assist the building's deterioration and smashed many of its fine stained glass windows. Although considerable local concern over the building's future was expressed, little was done until a local doctor purchased the property and donated it to the San Bernardino County Museum Association for use as a museum.

Unfortunately, plans never materialized and it began to appear as if nobody really cared enough to save the structure. Recently, however, it has been transferred to the City of Rialto and the newly formed Rialto Historical Society to be used as a cultural center and museum. One hopes that this is where the buck stops!

ENTRY GATE • ST. MALO

St. Malo

AN EXCLUSIVE ENCLAVE

Pasadena, even in the 1920's was hot and smoggy during the summer months and many residents yearned for the cooling breezes along the coast. So, in 1926 Louise and Kenyon Keith founded the exclusive St. Malo settlement in Oceanside, primarily for the richer Pasadena families. Architectural controls were absolutely rigid, requiring half-timbered structures with high pitched roofs reminiscent of English Tudor or French Provincial styles. Sales of property were equally well controlled and potential new owners had to be approved by current residents.

Even today this town-within-a-town has a very select feel about it. There is only one entrance and although normally unguarded, the movements of strangers are closely monitored by wary residents!

MISSION ENTRANCE
SAN JUAN CAPISTRANO

San Juan Capistrano

THE UNLUCKY MISSION

This mission, founded in 1776 by Father Junipero Serra, was the seventh to be established in California. Unfortunately it has experienced a hazardous history beginning in 1812 when the main church was destroyed by a major earthquake which killed most of the worshippers including forty converted Indians. The church boasted a fine seven-dome structure built by skilled stone masons, some of whom were specially invited from Spain to assist in the construction.

A later attempt in 1865 to rebuild the walls of the huge church with adobe brick also met with disaster. This time the destruction came as a result of torrential rainstorms which washed away large sections of the building.

It seemed apparent to the friars at that time that God wasn't too keen on the idea of a seven-domed church, so the structure was left in ruins and services held in the narrow Serra Chapel. The chapel is claimed to be the oldest building in California and the only remaining church in the State used by that sturdy Majorcan, Junipero Serra. The narrowness of the building is a curious but necessary feature due to the relatively short-length timber available in the area at that time.

San Juan today is a tourist town with all the standard trimmings and its main claim to fame is the loyal swallows which return punctually every year on the fast day of St. Joseph (March 19) and depart on the date of the death of the Patron Saint of the Missions, St. John of Capistrano (October 23). The Mission guide book states modestly that this is believed to be coincidental.

RAILROAD STATION • SAN JUAN CAPISTRANO

MA DIXON'S RESTAURANT · VAL VERDE

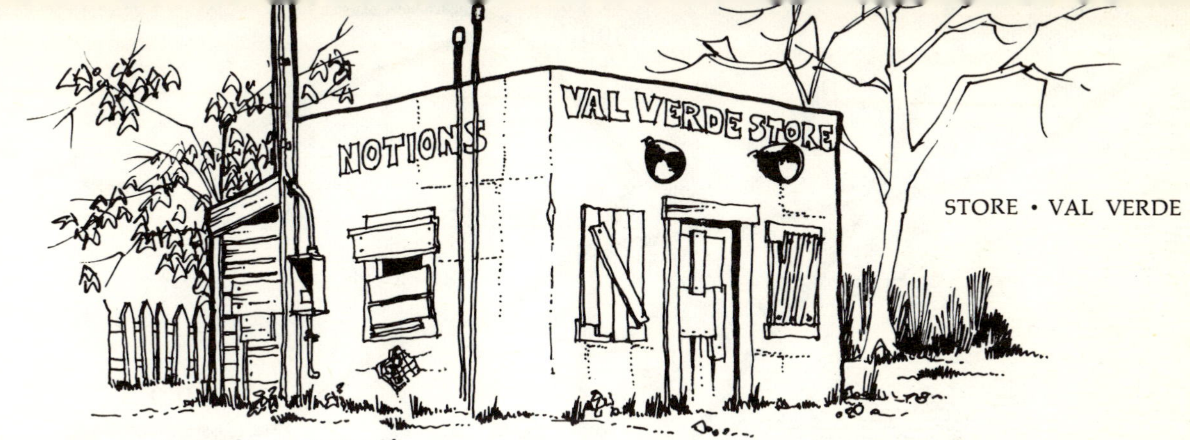

Val Verde

A SOUL-FOOD CENTER

In secluded isolation, the small straggling town of Val Verde nestles in the narrow San Martinez valley a few miles west of Freeway 5 and Route 126 junction. There are conflicting stories about its origins. Some claim it was founded to house workers employed in the nearby oil fields of the Santa Clara Valley. Others suggest more romantic associations and claim it began as a small resort community away from the over-crowded Los Angeles sprawl. Whatever the reason, Val Verde today is a sad remnant of a once flourishing little town. The old store, a perfect stucco cube, is boarded up and falling into disrepair. Just up the road is Ma Dixon's once famous soul food restaurant, a topsy-like complex of buildings centered around two old street cars which formed the main dining area. That too is closed and Ma Dixon herself, a local figure of some renown, passed away a short while ago. Charlie Marable, who runs a small restaurant nearby, continues to prepare hot links and barbecue dinners at weekends but admits he is no match for Ma Dixon's culinary skills.

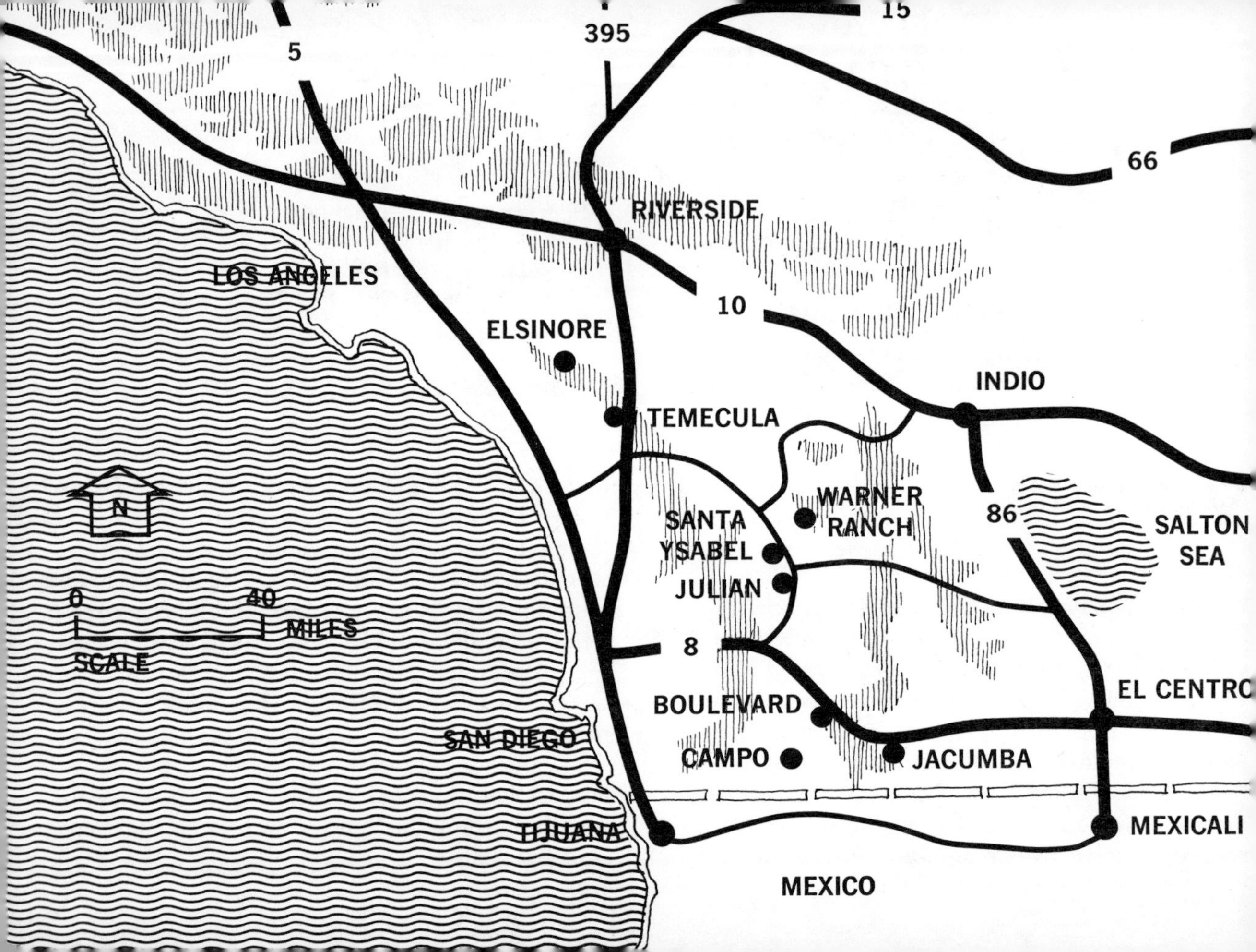

5
395
15
66
RIVERSIDE
LOS ANGELES
10
ELSINORE
INDIO
TEMECULA
N
WARNER RANCH
86
SANTA YSABEL
SALTON SEA
JULIAN
0
40
MILES
SCALE
8
BOULEVARD
EL CENTRO
SAN DIEGO
CAMPO
JACUMBA
TIJUANA
MEXICALI
MEXICO

The Back Country

The exploration of the Spaniard, Gaspar de Portola, coupled with the missionary efforts of Father Junipero Serra, a Majorcan, led to the discovery and early colonization of the southwestern sector of California. The mission centers at San Luis Rey, San Juan Capistrano, San Diego and San Gabriel were supported by *asistencias* (branch missions) and mission ranchos, usually located in the back country away from the coastal areas. Following the Mexican revolt against Spanish influence in 1821 a gradual secularization of the missions took place during which many of the ranchos and *asistencias* were abandoned and eventually granted to individuals by the civil authorities.

Following California's emergence as a State of the Union on September 9, 1850, and the discovery of gold in the northern Sierras, settlers poured in by the thousands. The famous Southern Immigrant Route passed through the center of the back country. Those were the days of wagon trains and scouts. Kit Carson, famous for his role in the battle between the Mexicans and the "army of the west" at San Pasqual in 1846, became one of the legendary figures of this era.

The shortlived Butterfield Stage, established by John Butterfield in 1858, clattered and jolted its way from Tucson to San Francisco through the back country. Aguanga, Temecula and Laguna (Elsinore) were then important stage posts. In 1869, however, the shortlived stage coach era declined with the completion of the Southern Pacific Railroad.

The next era of development in the back country resulted from the discovery of gold, tin and other ores in the area. Many of the old mining settlements such as those associated with the Lost Soldier and Lost Horse mines are merely names on old maps today. However, some settlements, such as Julian and Banner, survived as agricultural centers.

As the major cities of San Diego, Los Angeles and San Bernardino began to flourish, the back country became a valuable supplier of livestock

CANDY STORE • BOULEVARD

and fruit for the fat urban bellies. In addition, the abundance of hot springs in the earthquake belt (which includes most of the back country) led to the growth of resort communities such as Jacumba, Elsinore and Murrieta. Although to some extent these communities have been by-passed with the growth of "neon desert resorts" at Palm Springs and Palm Desert, they still exist and await the development of new freeway links to bring about their Twentieth Century renaissance.

In contrast to the dry, searing desert in the east and the overcrowded coastline to the west, the back country is quiet, green and full of hidden surprises. Tiny towns hide in secluded valleys. Narrow country roads wander through woods and between high mountain peaks. Small farms still reflect the days of the Mexican ranchos. However, the area may not remain this way for long. Already the mammoth metropolitan cities are encroaching upon its fringes and mobile home sites speckle the slopes for many miles east of San Diego.

Go and enjoy the back country while there's still time.

Boulevard

A CANDY STORE PAR EXCELLENCE

U.S. Highway 80, as it passed over the In-Co-Pah Mountains on its way to the Imperial Valley, once boasted a whole string of communities with esoteric names such as Whitestar, Rainbow City, Oak Knowles, Mistletoe Lodge, Bankhead Springs (recently a notice there read "Town for Sale"!) and Boulevard. Today little remains of these places except the delightfully rustic Wisteria Candy Cottage.

Founded in 1921, the tiny store does an amazing trade in homemade candy including nut clusters, English toffee, pecan roll, chop suey brittle, stuffed dates, Wisteria brittle, rocky road and 17 kinds of divinity! One local resident remarked "The Wisteria keeps the Post Office going!" It must as there's hardly anything else around!

Campo

A FAMOUS GUN-FIGHT

In the late 1800's the Mexican borderland was a notorious region for *bandidos*. The proximity of Mexico and the almost impassable nature of the mountainous scrublands made it hard to capture the cunning bands of Mexicans who murdered, looted and pillaged the area at frequent intervals.

Silas and Lumen Gaskill, who ran the store, bar, blacksmith shop, mill, post office and hotel in the small town of Campo, just north of the border, vowed that no *bandidos* would ever raid their tiny empire. With the help of willing residents they constructed this virtually impregnable mini-fort with boulders from nearby hillsides and laid in a large enough supply of guns and ammunition to withstand a major siege.

Most *bandidos* skirted the town at a respectful distance. However Pancho Lopez, one of the original Tiburcio Vasquez gang, vowed to take Campo and along with a band of six gunmen attacked the sturdy fort on December 4, 1875.

Although Silas and Lumen were taken by surprise, a furious gang battle ensued in which most of the Lopez gang were wiped out or captured. Lopez is said to have had reinforcements ready in the hills around the town, but they turned and fled.

From that time onward, Campo slumbered peacefully in its little hollow beside a rocky stream.

OLD CAMPO STORE · CAMPO

THE CHIMES · ELSINORE

Elsinore

"A STRICTLY TEMPERATE AND MORAL COMMUNITY"

The Elsinore Colony founded around 1885 by Franklin Heald, offered land to moderate income families. The land around Pasadena and Riverside was already too expensive! The sales brochure set the tone for development . . .

"Elsinore is a strictly temperate and moral community. We encourage schools, religious, literary and temperance societies and discourage and discountenance any attempts at saloons."

The town boasted a lake (the Indians called it Estenguo Wumoma), hot mineral springs and local industry built around clay and coal mining. The magnificent hotel and spa—now an antique store called The Chimes—became the social center of the valley.

The growth of the film industry in Hollywood led to Elsinore's first major boom. The famous evangelist singer, Aimee Semple McPherson had herself a Moorish castle built high on the slopes above the lake and many other stars found the town an attractive escapist center.

However, the development of Palm Springs and a dwindling lake level led to a slump. In 1951 the lake disappeared altogether! Fortunately large supplies of underground water were found and coupled with water drawn from the Colorado River, these serve to keep the lake level steady.

Today Elsinore is a popular resort community but many of its older residences, particularly those along the lake shore, have long since vanished.

HOTEL JACUMBA • JACUMBA

Jacumba

SPA TOWN WITH A CHINESE CASTLE

The town began in 1852 as a stage post on the
main road between Yuma and San Diego—the
Old Plank Road. This road was made entirely out

CHINESE CASTLE • JACUMBA

of wooden planks and crossed the famous sand dune belt west of Yuma—an area often called the American Sahara. By the way, if you cross those dunes at night and come upon a ghostly camel train led by a little man in a fez—locally known as Haji Ali—don't panic. Just stop the car and wave. He'll wave back! Legend has it the camels are the remains of the herd imported for use by the U.S. Camel Corps stationed at Fort Tejon in the 1860's.

The real development of Jacumba occurred early this century when local hot springs were found. The grandiose hotel was built in 1927, along with the equally ornate spa buildings. During World War II, the town formed part of an army camp and was by all local accounts—a hell of a rip-roaring place. One army officer settled here with his Chinese war bride and built a superb Chinese Castle on a rocky hill overlooking the town.

LIBRARY · JULIAN

Julian

THE HANDSOME MIKE JULIAN

Mike Julian was a ladies man *par excellence*. The town was almost called Bailey after Mike's cousins James and Frank Bailey. However, they magnanimously decided that as Mike was by far the most handsome and popular of the group, the town should be named after him. In addition to the school district and the mining district, even James Madison's record breaking quarter horse was christened Mike Julian. Mike eventually retired to Long Beach where he opened an hotel— The Julian Hotel—of course.

In 1868 the Baileys and Julians found gold which led to a series of rushes into the area. Another group, arriving a year or so later, found a rich quartz and gold ledge close to the town. The ledge was found on a Sunday and could not be registered until the following day. That particular Monday happened to be Washington's birthday and the mine thus became known as the

MAIN STREET • JULIAN

MESA GRANDE MISSION

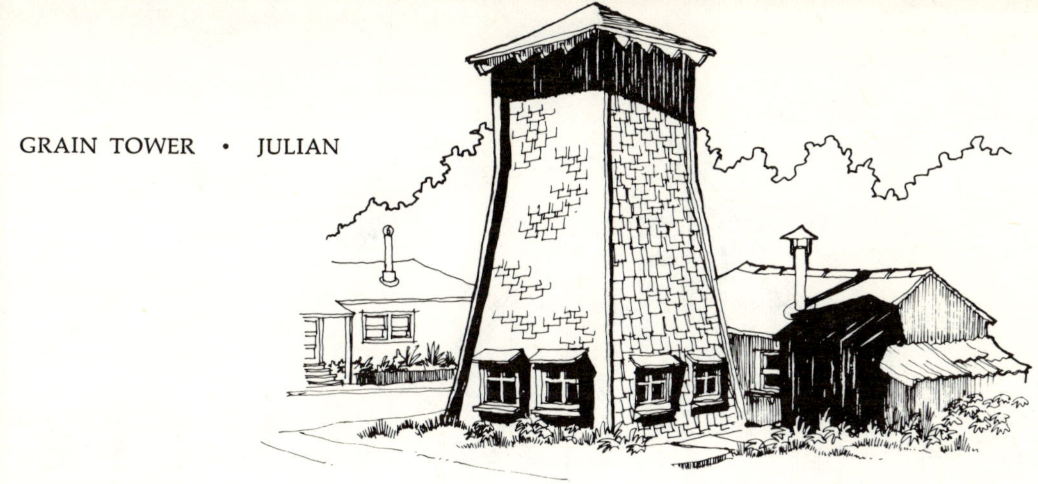

Washington Mine—one of the richest and most famous in the area.

Julian's inaccessible position created problems at first. Supplies had to be hauled in by pack mule over rough mountain tracks until a toll road was eventually built linking Julian to Santa Ysabel and the Spencer Valley. Eventually Wells Fargo established an express office in the booming town, the Julian Hotel was built, and a stage line set up to San Diego.

As with many gold-boom settlements, the ore was worked too fast and the elaborate plans for the development of the town as a major agricultural and resort center never materialized.

Julian today is a quiet, charming place, well-known for its apple orchards. Many of the old buildings still remain, including the school (now a library). Actually the school was imported intact from nearby Witch Creek. Behind the main street are a few of the old tall grain storage sheds, now mostly unused.

A few miles away, high up in an alpine-like valley, sits the Mesa Grande Mission which is a fine example of simple early Californian architecture.

BARN · SANTA YSABEL

Santa Ysabel

BARNS AND BAKERIES

The town grew as a trading center for the Spencer Valley and was named after the mission located nearby. In addition to the general store (supposedly founded in 1870) and one of the finest barns in the back country, the town possesses a superb bakery which produced, at last count, 50 different varieties of bread—using recipes collected from all over the world.

GENERAL STORE · SANTA YSABEL

Temecula

The Indians called it Temeku—"the place where the sun breaks through and shines in a white mist." Close by, up the Pauma Valley, is the scene of the 1847 Indian massacre when the Cahuilla tribe, led by some of General Pio Pico's men, slaughtered most of the Pauma and Temecula tribes.

The town has shifted around quite a bit. Evidence suggests that 7000 years ago (!) there was a settlement located a mile or so south of the existing town. With the establishment of the Butterfield Stage Route in 1858, a second Temecula was founded about three miles to the east. Finally with the introduction of the railroad (1882) it moved to its present position.

Located within the straggle of wooden false front stores are two old hotels, the magnificent Temecula and the more restrained Stallion. The Stallion, originally named the Ramona Inn (after the novel *Ramona* by Helen Hunt Jackson), was once run by Joe Winkels (the sage of Temecula) who was an ardent boxing fan. Part of the second floor of the hotel was converted into a boxing ring and regular visitors included Ad Wolgast and Jack Dempsey.

Until 1915 Temecula was famous for its granite which now adorns the Riverside County Courthouse and once formed the curbstones of Market Street in San Francisco. The large monument to many of the West's folk figures which stands on the edge of town is a piece of Temecula granite.

Before its pioneering days drew to a close, Temecula had one other claim to fame—its blacksmith was given the dubious honor of being the last person legally hanged in the State of California.

HOTEL TEMECULA • TEMECULA

WARNER RANCH

Warner Ranch

JUAN JOSE WARNER

The old adobe-built Warner Ranch is in a state of disrepair but when it was built in 1845 it was one of the sturdiest structures in the area. John Trumbull Warner originally came to California in 1831 to buy mules to take back to Louisiana. However he stayed and married the foster sister of Governor Pio Pico (the last Mexican Governor of California) and was granted the 48,000 acre valley of San Jose. Appropriately he became a Mexican citizen, thereafter known as Juan Jose Warner.

The ranch became a well-known halting place on the southern immigrant trail. Once the settlers got to Warner Ranch after the long trek across the desert, they knew they'd made it. In 1846 General Kearny passed through after the Battle of San Pasqual and in 1848 Warner just escaped with his life when local Indians, encouraged by his farm manager, Bill Marshall, ransacked the building. In 1858 the ranch became a station on the Butterfield Mail route and was later leased by the empire-building Walter Vail after whom the nearby Vail Lake was named.

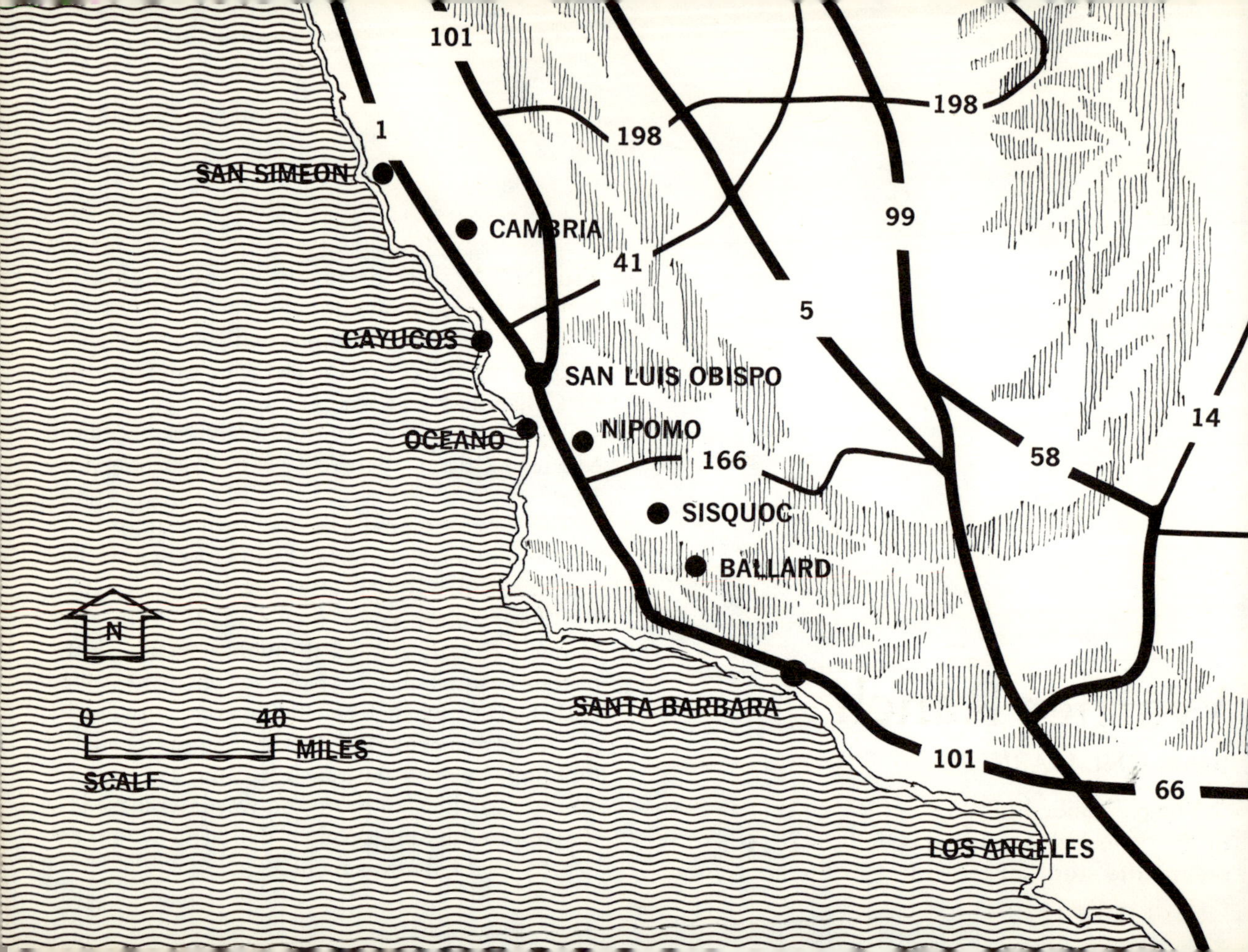

101
198
198
1
SAN SIMEON
CAMBRIA
99
41
5
CAYUCOS
SAN LUIS OBISPO
OCEANO
NIPOMO
166
14
SISQUOC
58
BALLARD
N
SANTA BARBARA
0
40
MILES
101
SCALE
66
LOS ANGELES

The Central Coast

Lantis, in his book *California, Land of Contrasts* (Wadsworth 1963), describes the Central Coast in the 1830's as the "idyllic time in California. Lands remained unfenced, the cattle roamed widely and the rancheros and their retainers indulged in numerous fiestas."

Prior to the 30's most of the land along the central coast had been in the hands of the zealous missionaries who, following Portola's exploration of the coastal fringe, established a string of regularly spaced missions from San Diego to San Francisco.

The missionaries' aim along the Central Coast was primarily the conversion of the Costanoan and Chumash Indians who lived close to the shore and in the Santa Ynez Mountains. Their work progressed smoothly until the termination of Spanish dominance in 1821 by the Mexicans and the secularization of the missions during 1834-36.

As in other parts of California, secularization brought about an inevitable boom of new "land grants." Along the coast, the mission herds formed the basis for extensive and rich cattle ranching during the 1835-50 period.

Then came trouble. In 1850 California became a State of the Union and all land grants made during the Mexican era had to be re-verified. To add to the confusion, many miners were leaving the "Mother Lode" goldfields to become farmers and

SCHOOL · BALLARD

along with the thousands of new immigrants from the east coast and mid-west, they "squatted" on lands which were, as far as they were concerned, "free."

By 1870 the "idyllic" rancho period was at an end and most of the large landholdings had been subdivided into smaller farms.

Agricultural trends fluctuated along the coast. At one period, during the Civil War, wool was a vital necessity and Basque sheepherders were a common sight throughout the coastal ranges. Then, following the completion of the Southern Pacific link from San Francisco to Los Angeles, the area's dairy potential attracted hundreds of Swiss, Danish and Portuguese farmers in addition to providing the impetus for a rash of coastal resorts for Los Angeles residents.

Today the central coast is still delightfully rural. Narrow country lanes run through tiny unspoiled villages like Ballard and Sisquoc. Even the larger settlements such as Cambria and Oceano still contain fascinating glimpses of country life as it must have been at the turn of the century.

Ballard

THE LITTLE RED SCHOOL HOUSE

Think of the days of horse-drawn buggies, Mom's home-made chicken 'n' dumplings and hymn-singing in church on Sunday and somehow, in your reminiscences of rural America, the proverbial little red school house with its one-room classroom and pot-bellied stove will come to mind.

Ballard, a tiny village just north of Solvang, has such a school, set back from the road and shaded by two huge trees. It was built in 1883 and has been used continuously as a school, community center and meeting place.

The central coast is rich in similar tiny schools and churches but the Ballard School House seems to represent the best of Early Californian wood architecture.

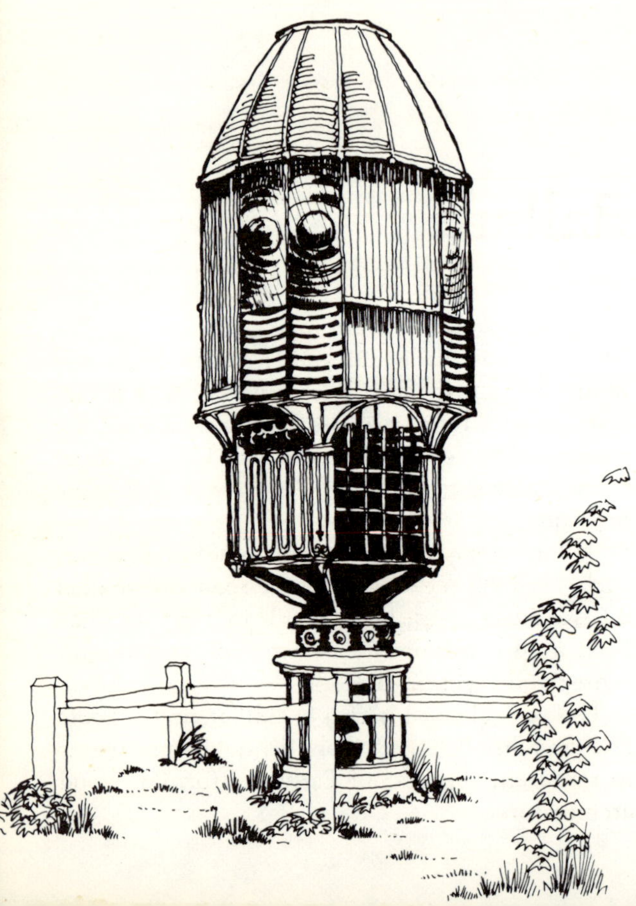

Cambria

THE CAPTAIN'S HOUSE

The town nestles in a wooded hollow—it's a sleepy place much reminiscent of an old New England village complete with shingled church and restrained carpenter-Gothic architecture.

A little less than a century ago, however, Cambria was the second largest town in San Luis Obispo County, with its own quicksilver mine and a prosperous farming and dairying industry, employing large numbers of Swiss and Italian immigrants. In 1871 the famous Excelsior Cheese factory was built near the town and local records show that, during its peak, Cambria exported as much as a ton of butter and half a ton of cheese daily to San Francisco by ship. Ships were guided past the Piedras Blancas Point by a beautiful lighthouse lamp, constructed by the French, which was in continuous operation from 1874-1949.

Today the tourist trade predominates, but high above the town, on a rough track, lives a man

BEALE HOUSE • CAMBRIA

who is saddened by Cambria's creeping commercialism. Arthur Beale, known locally as The Captain, started building his unique Gaudi-influenced house in the 1920's and is still extending it up the rocky hillside. The main building materials seem to consist of pebbles, abalone shells, odd planks of wood and Victorian bric-a-brac. But somehow it all holds together!

Cayucos

ONCE FAMOUS FOR BAKED CLAMS

Cayucos is well and truly by-passed by Route 1 and has managed to keep its seaside village character. The town's unusual name originates from 1542 when Juan Cabrillo and his exploring party found a small Indian village in the bay and named the place Cayucos after an Indian term meaning skin canoes.

In 1867 an English sailor, James Cass, took over the Morro y Cayucos Rancho and built himself this fine home with the lumber specially transported from San Francisco by ship. He also constructed a wharf which started a minor boom in the adjoining rich agricultural areas and attracted a large number of Swiss farmers.

Cass, however, lost interest in farming and returned to the sea and it took C. H. Phillips, the first real estate promoter of San Luis Obispo County, to realize the development potentials of the area and set out to subdivide the remainder of the old rancho. By 1890 the town boasted this fine old hotel renowned for its famous baked clams. Today the hotel is empty.

OLD HOTEL · CAYUCOS

DANA HOUSE • NIPOMO

Nipomo

HOME OF THE DANA FAMILY

The delicately-styled Dana house is today an antique store but once housed part of the famous Dana family, the original settlers in the area in 1834. Captain William Dana raised great herds of cattle on his ranch, but due to increasing decimation by drought, he turned to wheat, barley and flax farming which according to local records, yielded mammoth proportions. Nipomo has a varied history. In its heyday it was considerably larger than nearby Santa Maria due to the Pacific Coast Railway which was constructed through the town in 1882, making it into a major agricultural rail stop.

Subsequently the ravages of fire (a common punctuation of most small town histories) and the increasing dominance of Santa Maria led to Nipomo's decline. Many of its original buildings were moved intact to Santa Maria.

Today the town is a sleepy remnant of its former self. Route 101, which used to bring some action to the town, now passes in freeway fashion to the west and the only life is provided by Jocko's restaurant — a rip-roaring steak-eater's paradise!

Oceano

THE VICTORIAN SPLENDOR OF OCEANO

Close to Oceano, which once was a major shipping center for produce from the Arroyo Grande Valley, is a large wind-swept area of grass-topped sand dunes. Somewhere deep under the dunes lie the remains of Le Grande Beach Pavilion erected in Victorian splendor in 1905. This was to be the main promotional element of a huge seaside recreation project known as Le Grande Beach. However, although 7,000 lots were sold, mainly by mail order, the creeping sand hampered all efforts to develop the area. By 1920 the project had been abandoned and the magnificent pavilion left to the ravages of vandals and the elements.

Oceano, however, still possesses two magnificent examples of late Victorian homes. The Coffee T. Rice house, which today is surrounded by a ghastly huddle of mobile homes, was built in 1885. Rice envisaged Oceano as a major industrial center on the coastal railroad. Unfortunately, the railroad was a long time coming and by the

ROSA HOUSE • OCEANO

SEBASTIAN STORE · SAN SIMEON

time the first train passed through, Rice, his fortunes depleted, had left.

The refined Parker-Davis house, built in 1886, is, in comparison, beautifully restored. Recently attempts have been made to convert it into a museum and a restaurant but Joe Rosa, its present owner, has turned it back into a private residence.

San Simeon
"KING" HEARST'S CASTLE

In the 1860's, San Simeon was a small Portuguese whaling station boasting a short pier, a cluster of wooden huts and a clapboard trading store out on the point. Today as a result of newspaper magnate William Randolph Hearst's uncompromising aesthetic taste, most of the buildings in the village are Spanish-styled with the exception of the false-front Sebastian's trading store which was moved intact to its present location just before the turn of the century.

Hearst's father, Senator George Hearst, originally purchased the Piedra Blanca land grant from Jose Pico in 1865 and created a highly productive ranch. However, it took his son—the notorious William Randolph—to create the massive Hearst Castle which now overlooks the village in magnificent splendor from its mountain site. Although the castle, named La Cuesta Encantada (the Enchanted Hill) by Hearst, is now owned by the State and open to the public, much of the surrounding ranch remains a part of the Hearst empire.

Although Hearst was once one of the richest men in America, he was strangely shy and aloof. Obituaries at the time of his death referred to him as an "elemental force" and "the greatest figure in American journalism" while others were more skeptical about this man who "set himself up as a king, owned 7 castles, looted the world of art and carried on a one-man war with France."

The mission styled building in the village is no more than a warehouse, constructed to store the numerous art treasures which Hearst imported from Europe to display in the Castle. Just across from the warehouse, in an overgrown field, sits a once-dainty one-roomed school which now is in a state of sad decay.

OLD SCHOOL · SAN SIMEON

Sisquoc

A WOODPECKERS' PARADISE

A few miles north of the famous Mission Santa Ynez in the small, unusual Danish town of Solvang, is this fragile village church near Sisquoc.

Built in 1875, the church is located on a steep bluff away from the main road and about a mile out of Sisquoc. In California it's unusual to find this separation of village and church although it's a relatively common feature in Europe, particularly if the church was built to serve a number of adjacent communities.

The two-tower design is also an uncommon feature although the old Catholic Church in Guadalupe, built around the same time, has a similar characteristic.

The building seems little used. Paint is flaking from the white wooden walls and woodpeckers use the main structural members for drilling practice.

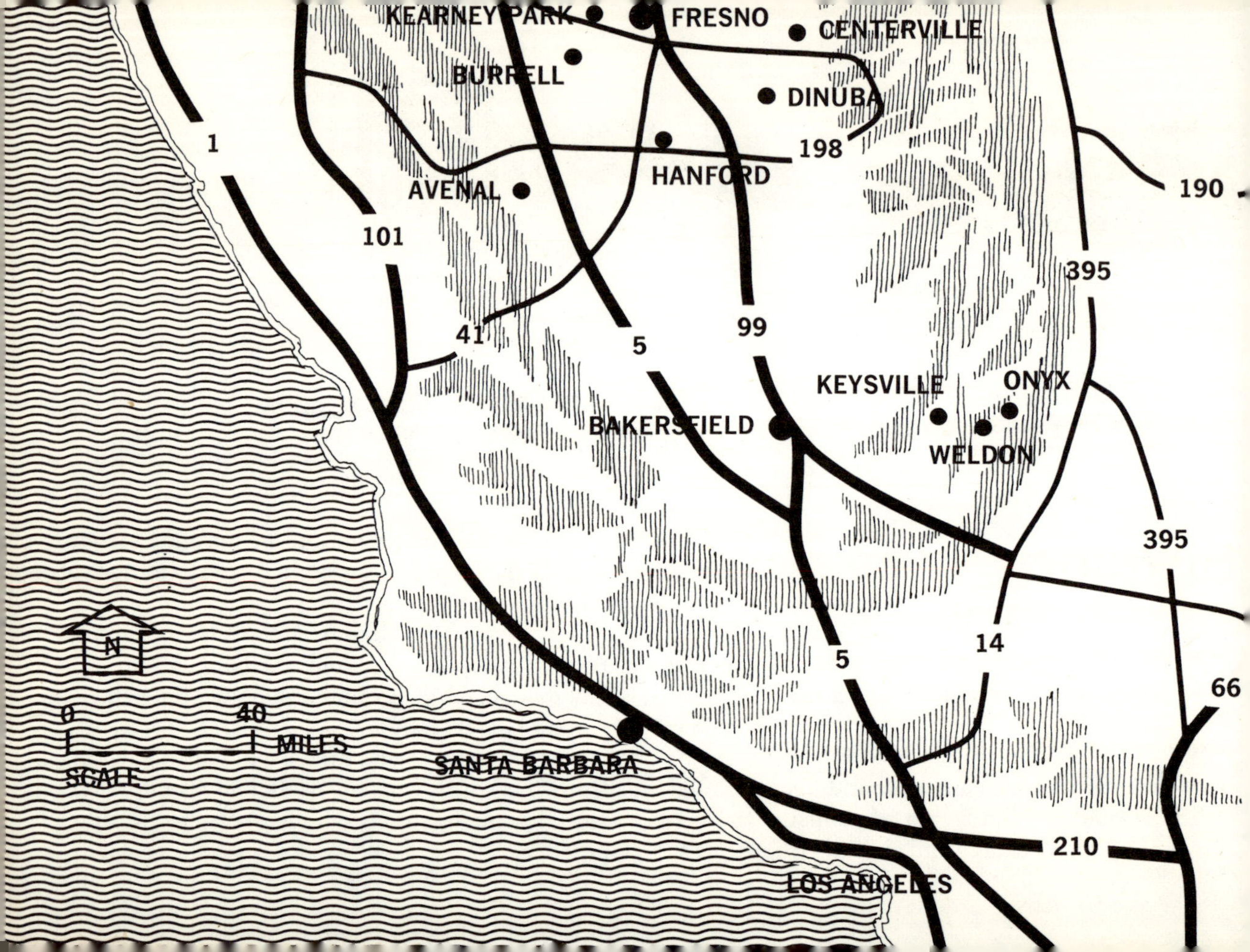

N
KEARNEY PARK
FRESNO
CENTERVILLE
BURRELL
DINUBA
1
198
HANFORD
AVENAL
190
101
395
41
5
99
KEYSVILLE
ONYX
BAKERSFIELD
WELDON
395
14
5
66
0
40
MILES
SCALE
SANTA BARBARA
210
LOS ANGELES

San Joaquin Valley and Sierras

Prior to the gold rush boom of the 1850's San Joaquin Valley was a harsh, brittle landscape which burned under the summer sun, flooded extensively during the Spring, was subjected to ferocious dust storms and clammy "tule fogs" and was the home of roaming bands of Miwok and Yokut Indians.

But in 1901, Frank Norris in his book *The Octopus* wrote of the San Joaquin Valley:

"The wheat, now close to its maturity, had turned from pale yellow to golden . . . like a gigantic carpet it spread itself all over the land. There was nothing else to be seen but the limitless sea of wheat."

The transition from desert to garden paradise was miraculous in its rapidity. Early development in the valley during the Spanish/Mexican period, however, had been marginal. Occasionally search parties were sent out in the scrublands to pursue escaped Indian converts but mainly missionary influence was concentrated along the narrow El Camino Viejo route, established along the western edge of the valley as a more speedy link between San Francisco and San Diego than the famous El Camino Real which followed the coast.

Although famous personalities of western folklore including Jedidiah Smith and Captain John C. Fremont had travelled extensively throughout the valley, it took the gold rush of '49 to stimulate profitable use of the valley's resources.

The gold rush towns—often located high up in the Northern Sierras—needed a constant supply of crops and meat to sustain their hearty residents. Thus within a short period, cattle ranches were established, usually without definite boundaries, all over the valley but particularly in the east where the more fertile land was to be found.

As the area prospered, many of the smaller ranches were taken over by rich landowners, including the famous team of Miller and Lux. Miller, at the time of his death, left his heirs over one million acres of land and one million cattle!

The slow decline of the gold rush towns coupled with the disastrous drought of 1863-4 brought a temporary halt to the boom and was instrumental in encouraging a switch from ranching to grain cultivation. The construction of the

Southern Pacific Valley Line in 1869 further encouraged agricultural development and by the 1880's more intensive irrigation agriculture was commonplace which gave the valley its famous title of "fruit basket of the world." Coordination of the valley's water resources, partial elimination of regular flooding from the Delta region in the 1940's and finally the discovery of vast supplies of oil in the area around Taft set the seal of the valley's prosperity.

The lower Sierra foothills, particularly around Kernville and Lake Isabella, developed somewhat later than the valley and it was not until the gold rush of the '60's that attention was drawn to this secluded, almost inaccessible sector of the State. Although the gold rush was relatively short-lived, the area's popularity increased and today it is one of the most charming resort areas in southern California.

Avenal

HOME OF THE "BLUE GOOSE"

On the outskirts of the town is this strange monument which commemorates the discovery of the vast Kettleman Hills North Dome Oil Field in October 1928. Known as a Christmas Tree it's a complex valve mechanism which was custom-designed for the North Dome Field to control the tremendous pressures and regulate the productive capacity of these early wells.

Almost immediately following the initial gushes a tent town sprang up on flat land just below the Dome, complete with tent theater! Subsequently the town and its theater evolved into more permanent structures and today this edifice stands as a splendid, but abandoned, reminder of the prosperous days of Avenal during the 30's and 40's. At that time the town was a pretty wild place with a generous share of bars and six pleasure houses, sporting names like the Red Onion and Blue Goose. Unfortunately, moral indignation and the proximity of military bases led to the closure of these worthy institutions during the Second World War.

THEATER · AVENAL

BURRELL ADOBE • BURRELL

Burrell

BLACK SHEEP AND ELKS

The San Joaquin Valley was once famous for its rich raucous English-born ranchers who often came from wealthy, titled families in the home-land—it being the custom in those days to dispose of black-sheep relatives in as face-saving a way as possible!

Whether English-born Cuthbert Burrell fell into such a category is questionable but in 1860 he became owner of the large, swampy Elkhorn Ranch named after the numerous elks which once roamed the area. Burrell's adobe ranch house, built largely by local Chinese labor, boasts 18" thick walls and still stands today on a wooded knoll overlooking the small town which bears his name. Although no longer the proud mansion it once was, the house is still well-maintained and used by farm workers and their families.

Farmyards in the area present a somewhat romantic picture of rural decay with their pedestalled water storage tanks, dilapidated farm wagons, old out-buildings and shaky artesian well pumps. This is a familar sight throughout the San Joaquin valley and the basilica form of the barns remains relatively unchanged throughout the whole area. It's amazing to think of the effort that must have gone into the construction of these buildings, particularly when wood was a scarce commodity in the valley.

Unfortunately, similar forms of decay in the towns are by no means romantic. The straggling town of Lanare, inhabited largely by blacks, is sad evidence of the poverty and living conditions of many of the valley's farmworkers.

FARMYARD • LANARE

RURAL SLUMS • LANARE

Centerville

THE OBSTINACY OF WILLIAM CALDWELL

If William Caldwell, one of the original land owners in the area, had been more cooperative with the President of the Central Pacific Railroad, Centerville would have undoubtedly become the County Seat and Fresno might not even exist today. However, as it was, Caldwell refused to make any concessions to the railroad company (a polite form of bribe) and thus Centerville today snoozes peacefully beside the Kings River.

Like many small towns in California, Centerville moved around quite a bit. Originally, in 1853, it was named Scottsburg after a colorful resident, Monte Scott, renowned as an Indian fighter and gambler. The town was located on the banks of the Kings River but after several damaging floods it was moved higher up on the bluffs and its name changed to Centerville.

The white, very woody Oddfellows Lodge is the only major building left in town, but just around the corner is the strange tower-like Moodey House, built for use as an artist's studio.

MOODEY HOUSE · CENTERVILLE

ODDFELLOWS HALL • CENTERVILLE

'WATERTOWER' HOUSE • DINUBA

Dinuba

WATER-TOWER HOUSES

No one really knows what Dinuba means, or why the town was so named. Some think it was after the Pronuba moth, a pest prevalent in the valley in the late 19th century. Others claim that James Sibley, the original owner of the area, named it after the famous Greek battlefield, however, no reference can be found anywhere to such a battlefield. The mystery remains.

Just outside the small town are a group of interesting farmhouses built around the turn of the century. They are unusual in that the water storage tank, usually located a distance away from the house, has been cleverly incorporated into the architecture of the buildings and is disguised as a delicate tower. Why this feature should be limited mainly to the Dinuba area, no one knows. Another mystery!

On the outskirts of Dinuba is this innovative mail box which forms an integral part of a small plough. Such pieces of folk-art are a familiar sight on the back roads of rural California.

MAILBOX · NEAR DINUBA

Hanford

A PRESERVED CHINATOWN

It was common custom for the pioneering railroad companies to name towns after their respected officials. Thus in the case of Hanford, the name of James A. Hanford is forever immortalized although most local inhabitants have no idea who the honored gentleman was or what he did, except that he was employed by Southern Pacific during the construction of the railroad through the town in 1876.

By 1883, Hanford, in common with many valley towns, possessed a flourishing Chinatown complete with noodle factory, opium dens, laundries, a Taoist temple, herbalists and fortune tellers. The Chinese were reluctant to give up their cultural and philosophical ties with their homeland (almost all the Chinese families in Hanford came from the Far-Yuen region near Canton) and they generally led an insular existence within the confines of their towns. This isolationist tendency, along with fears of a Chinese takeover in California, led to appalling massacres, the pas-

The First and Oldest
L. T. SUE HERB CO.
L. T. SUE CO.
HERB STORE
HANFORD

sage of highly discriminatory legislation and a gradual disintegration of oriental communities.

By 1953 Hanford's Chinatown was virtually deserted and it is only slowly coming back to life, albeit in the somewhat sterile form of a tourist attraction.

Kearney Park
THE FRUSTRATIONS OF THEO KEARNEY

M. Theo Kearney wrote his own sad epitaph which reads:

"Here lies the body of M. Theo Kearney, a visionary who thought he could teach the average farmer . . . some of the rudiments of sound land management.

For 8 years he worked strenuously at his task and at the end of that time he was no further ahead than in the beginning.

The effort killed him."

Kearney is thought to have been born in Liverpool, England early in the 19th century. In 1842 he came to San Francisco and soon became a trusted employee of W. S. Chapman, a wealthy land speculator, who eventually over-extended his company and went bankrupt. Kearney purchased his land holdings in the San Joaquin Valley at a ridiculously low price and was soon one of the wealthiest landowners in Fresno County. On his huge estate known as Fruit Vale he built this refined mansion which, ironically, was only intended to be the caretakers house. Kearney planned his own "Chateau Fresno" (modelled after Chateau Chenonceaux in France) a short distance away. However, when he died its construction had hardly started.

Kearney's pet concern was the valley raisin-growers whom he tried to form into a cooperative association in order to increase profits and unify production techniques. In 1898 he was elected president and during subsequent years was continually resigning and being begged to return.

He finally tired of the sad fiasco, convinced himself that all his work had been wasted and died alone in his stateroom during a transatlantic voyage in 1906.

REMNANTS OF KEYSVILLE

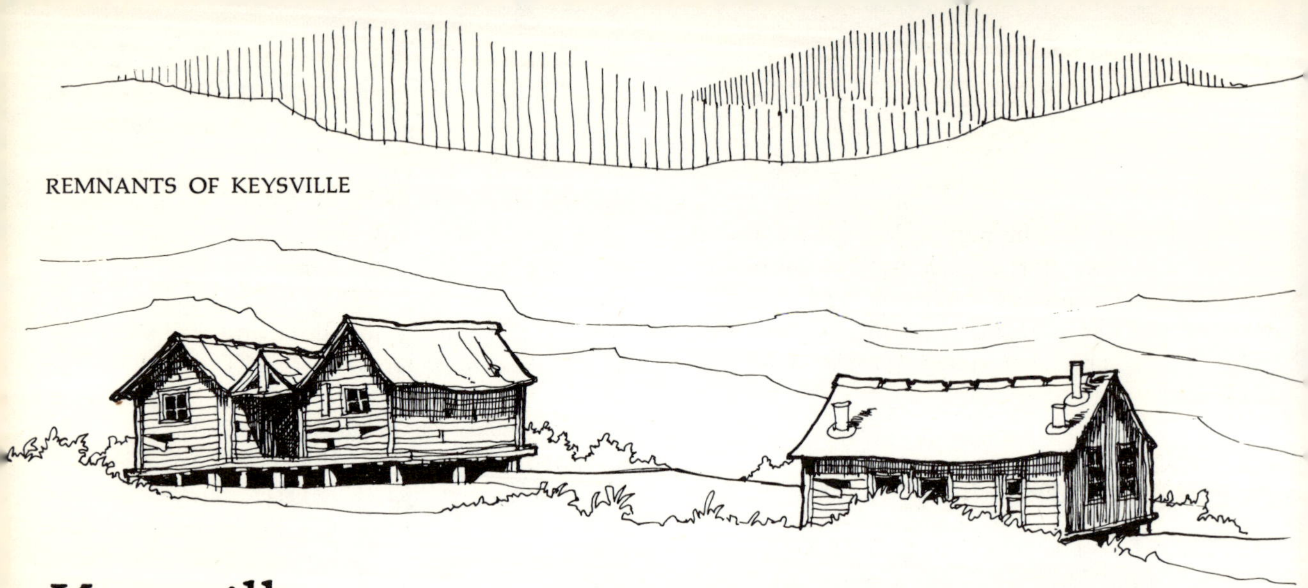

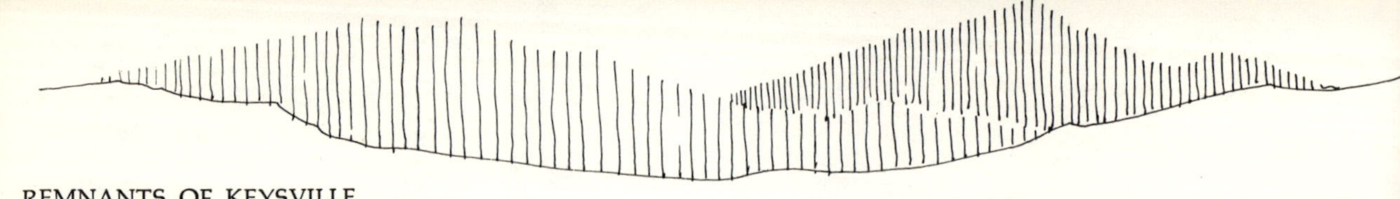

Keysville

THE LEGEND OF LOVELY ROGERS

Closely following the Mother Lode gold boom that gripped California and the world in 1849 came the lesser but equally frantic boom in the southern Sierra Nevadas. Hundreds of miners poured in from other claims that had started to dwindle and tent towns sprang up with names like Quartzburg, Whiskey Flat (later Kernville), Havilah and Keysville. Equally bizarre were the names of the prospectors, particularly that of Lovely Rogers who, according to local legend, found the richest ore ledge along the north fork of the Kern.

Today Keysville, which once boasted an elaborate earthworks fortification against Indian attacks, is a rough patch of hilly scrub land with a few scattered buildings—a faint reminder of the past.

Onyx

HOTEL FOR FILM STARS

With its flimsy false front peering out from behind two magnificent Balm of Gilead trees, the Onyx Store looks just too much like an old western general store to be true. However, records show that it was built in the 1850's by pioneer rancher William Scodie, after whom a nearby portion of the Sierra Nevadas is named and that with the exception of an adjoining hotel which burnt down in 1935, the building has remained unchanged for almost 120 years. By all accounts the hotel was well patronized, and a glance through the old register reveals such guests as Charlie Chaplin, Jean Harlow, Douglas Fairbanks Jr., and Mary Pickford.

The store has seen its share of folklore. In 1863, an ox train passing nearby was attacked by Piute Indians with a loss of two settlers. A little later, Scodie himself was bound and gagged by the famous California bandit, Vasquez, who helped himself to merchandise and money from the store.

The store's current claim to fame is its homemade sausage which is known throughout the region.

ONYX STORE • ONYX

WATER
MELONS
ORANGES
OPEN
WATER
CANTA
GRAPE
TANGE

Strange Stores and Fruit Stands

FOLK ARCHITECTURE

Dotted throughout the valley are dozens of ticky-tacky fruit stands, some of them true masterpieces in folk architecture with their bright misspelt signs, wobbly display stands loaded with ripe fruit and flapping canvas awnings. Each one is unique. This one is located somewhere east of Fresno.

In addition to fruit stands, many of the smaller towns boast their own bric-a-brac stores bursting with second-hand furniture, stoves, refrigerators, clothing, books and other miscellaneous paraphernalia including the rather odd items sketched above. For many of the poorer families in the valley these places are invaluable. For the tourist they provide a fascinating diversion.

STORE • DOS PALOS

OLD FLOUR MILL • WELDON

Weldon

THE WEALTHY BROWNS

Weldon was well situated for its pioneer role at the fork of the Walker Pass route and the freight route to Los Angeles. The town was founded in 1867 by William Weldon, a pioneer stockman, and by the 1890's it was the social, cultural and spiritual center of the south fork area.

Across the fields from the old false-front store which sits by the main road is the magnificent old Brown & Co. flour mill. The activities of the Brown family in the area included ranching, general stores in Havilah, Old Kernville (now submerged under Lake Isabella) and Weldon, and a stage line which ran to the once famous mining town of Caliente near Tehachapi. Although the mill is generally in a state of disrepair, some of the old machinery still exists within the main building.

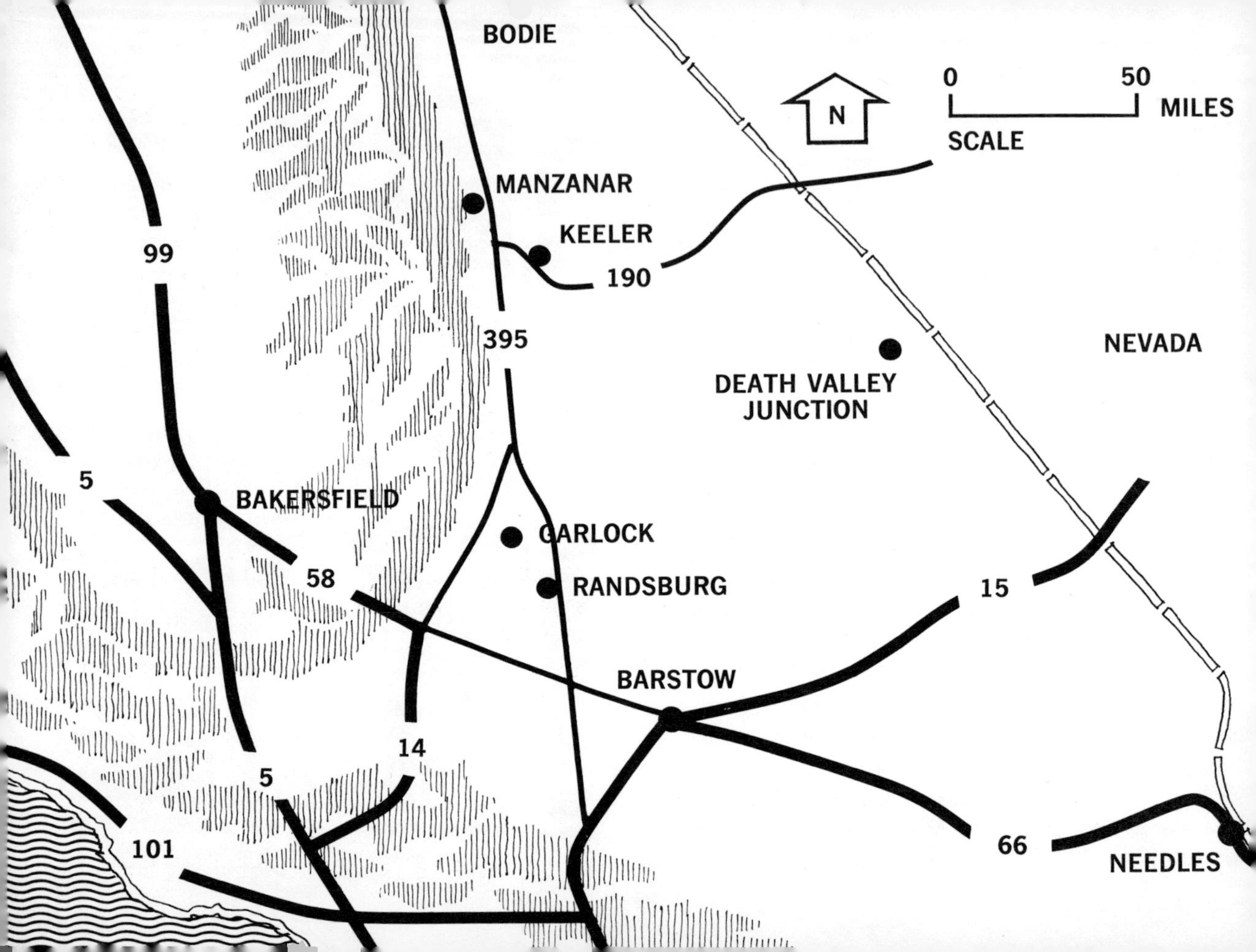

BODIE
MANZANAR
KEELER
190
99
395
NEVADA
DEATH VALLEY JUNCTION
5
BAKERSFIELD
58
GARLOCK
RANDSBURG
15
BARSTOW
14
5
101
66
NEEDLES
N
0
50
MILES
SCALE

The Desert

Mary Austin, author of *The Land of Little Rain*, writes lovingly of the desert:

"Painted lizards slip in and out of rock crevices and pant on the hot white sands. Birds, hummingbirds even, nest in the cactus scrub; woodpeckers befriend the demoniac yuccas; out of the stark, treeless waste rings the music of the night singing mocking bird. Strange, furry, tricksy things dart across the open places, or sit motionless in the conning towers of the creosote."

The first rash of settlements in the desert were the result of gold and silver finds of Cerro Gordo, Bodie, Darwin, Panamint, Calico and Rand during the 1860-70 period. Most mines were short-lived and far less spectacular than those in the Sierra mother-lode country. However, one mine in particular—the Harmony Borax mine in Death Valley, founded in 1882—was more permanent due largely to the efforts of "Borax Bill" Parkinson. His famous 20-mule wagon train regularly hauled 20 tons of borax from Death Valley to the railhead at Mojave along a rough route flattened by hundreds of diligent Chinese laborers—working with sledge hammers! Eventually, even

"Borax Bill's" efforts were overridden by economical considerations and the Harmony Mine was replaced by a larger concern at Boron.

The spaghetti of railroads laid during the mining era included the charming "Bullfrog and Goldfield Line" and the no-nonsense "Borate and Daggett Line." The poetic "Tonopah and Tidewater Line" was well-intentioned, but the boom ran out prior to its construction.

Agricultural development was limited only to those areas where a ready supply of water could be guaranteed—along the Colorado, in the Mojave River Valley and Owens River area. The latter was a flourishing agricultural center until the Los Angeles Water Right Purchase in 1904 which virtually turned the area back to desert scrub.

Desert development stagnated until the late 1940's when the Federal Government began to locate major bases throughout the area. The towns of China Lake and Ridgecrest appeared almost overnight as a result of the Naval Weapons Center in the Panamint Range area. Similar developments occurred at Ft. Irwin and Edwards.

Coupled with this sudden burst of activity in the desert, the Federal Government encouraged

MAIN STREET · BODIE

filings for small 5-acre holdings, particularly in the Lucerne and Morongo Valleys, Joshua Tree and Twenty Nine Palms. Today these areas are characterized by sprinklings of "Jack rabbit homesteads" and rigidly straight subdivision tracks across the arid wastelands. Such haphazard development coupled with the increasing use of off-road recreation vehicles pose dangerous threats to the delicately balanced desert ecology.

Bodie

"GOODBYE GOD, I'M GOING TO BODIE"

Bodie defies adjectives but try: highest (10,000 feet), coldest (—20 degrees has been recorded), drunkest (65 saloons), deadliest (a killing a day on average) and richest (one small claim produced $90,000 in two months).

An overworked vicar, the Reverend F. M. Warrington, described Bodie in its prime as "a sea of sin, lashed by the tempests of lust and passion." He could, of course, have been describing just

METHODIST CHURCH • BODIE

CEMETERY · BODIE

about any gold mining town during the boom era but from all accounts, Bodie was an exceptionally vibrant and virile community.

A little known prospector, Waterman S. Body, first discovered gold in the bleak windswept high desert north of Mono Lake in 1859. For many years little interest was shown in the area until the Mother Lode claims were exhausted. Then hundreds of miners poured into Bodie from all over the State and by 1879 the town bulged with a population of over ten thousand.

Bodie quickly developed all the characteristics of a typical mining town. It had its own Chinatown complete with joss house, opium dens, the Tong Association, laundries and tiny stores. Nearby was the red-light district with its appropriately named streets: Maiden Lane, Virgin Alley and Bonanza Street! The town supported three breweries and a host of fine saloons including Sawdust Corner, the Gymnasium and The Rifle Club, not to mention a French restaurant, *La Maison Doree*, which was renowned throughout the whole region for its quail in aspic!

At one point in its history, Bodie's main street was a solid mile of false-front buildings. Today it

CAIN HOUSE • BODIE

contains a handful of remnants similar to ones shown in the sketch.

James Stuart Cain, whose residence is one of the most imposing buildings remaining today, was the town's principal property owner and made his fortune initially from hauling in lumber across Mono Lake for the mines and later from operating a mine himself.

The cemetery, located half a mile from the town, only contains the "respectable" residents of Bodie. Others were buried in nearby *boot hill*, usually without markers. Most of the "badmen from Bodie" are interred here.

Death Valley Junction

BALLET IN THE BOONDOCKS

Death Valley Junction was built around 1923 as a borax company town and was fully equipped with rail head and Spanish-styled shops, hotel, offices and executive houses. In 1945 the company moved and Junction became, for a while,

OPERA HOUSE • DEATH VALLEY JUNCTION

the first 20th century ghost town in California. However, it survived and today the old commercial plaza is being revitalized by an art and craft center, a boutique and—believe it or not—an Opera House.

The Amargosa Opera House is a creation of Marta Becket—an artist and dancer. Each week during the winter, Marta dances three different programs of ballet-mime. In addition she and her husband have decorated the inside of this tiny building in 16th century Spanish style, with a whole royal audience, complete with king, queen and ladies of court painted on the walls.

Garlock

SHORTEST-LIVED TOWN IN CALIFORNIA

A barrage of No Trespassing and Keep Out signs provide a not too welcome indication of the remains of Garlock. The town is situated on the north slope of the El Paso Mountains close to Randsburg and was established in 1896 by Eugene Garlock who constructed a stamp mill for crushing gold ore from the Randsburg mines. It was short-lived. By 1898 the town lost much of its importance when local water was diverted to Randsburg and the Kramer-Randsburg Railroad was completed. A few buildings remain, including this gem constructed from old railroad ties.

OLD RAILROAD STATION · KEELER

Keeler

AN INLAND PORT FOR PADDLE STEAMER

All that is left of this bleached little town on the east bank of Owens Lake is the Carson and Colorado Railway Station, a few houses and community buildings, an old rail coach now converted into a dwelling and the inevitable U.S. post office.

Keeler is located close to the landing stage for the Bessie Bradie—a paddle steamer! The boat was launched in 1872 on Owens Lake to carry charcoal and supplies from the west bank to miners working the Cerro Gordo field! Sherman Stevens organized the whole operation. Flumes brought lumber from the west-facing slopes of the Sierras around Mount Whitney down to the valley floor where it was converted into charcoal in special mud built kilns and then dispatched across the lake.

By the time Keeler was founded in 1878, the minefields were almost worked out. Soda from Owens Lake became the next major industry. A special narrow gauge railroad was constructed from Carson City to Keeler to capitalize on an

CHARCOAL KILNS • NEAR OLANCHA

unexpected mining boom in the north Owens Valley and Mono area. The boom never materialized and the Carson and Colorado Railroad sold out to Southern Pacific in 1900. In 1959 the line was closed due to "declining and unpredictable use of line." Fortunately, however, the depot at Laws (near Bishop) is being retained as a railroad museum.

Although mining continues around Owens Lake today, Keeler lost much of its significance when the railroad closed. Its population of 100 is mainly retired but a number commute to nearby Lone Pine.

Manzanar

A FORGOTTEN COMMUNITY

On May 8th, 1942, the County of Los Angeles issued a special announcement to all persons of Japanese ancestry:

"Pursuant to the provisions of civilian exclusion order No. 54 all persons of Japanese ancestry, both aliens and non-aliens, will be evacuated . . . by 12 o'clock noon, May 14th, 1942."

Within a short period of time, 10,000 Japanese were living beneath the shadow of Mount Whitney in a special rehabilitation camp called by its local name—Manzanar. Today nothing is left of the town, located about 6 miles south of Independence, except an oriental-style entrance gate off the main highway. Souvenirs of the camp days in the form of intricately designed Japanese tea pots, saki warmers and camp newspapers printed in Japanese script, are on display at the Eastern California Museum in Independence.

REMAINS OF MANZANAR CAMP

MAIN STREET • RANDSBURG

Randsburg

THE TOWN THAT WOULDN'T DIE

Hidden from the main road (395) which passes through its more prosperous partner-city Johannesburg, Randsburg has retained much of its old character. From a distance it still looks like those old photographs of early mining settlements with tiny buildings scattered randomly across a bleak hillside and a main street of false-front stores and saloons.

The Rand area has experienced three distinct mining booms. The first began in 1895 when three prospectors—Mooers, Singleton and Burcham— found gold flakes in the lower *arroyos* of the Rand Mountains and, tracing these back to their source, discovered one of the richest single mines in southern California—the Yellow Aster. Within a few weeks a straggling tent town had sprung up, fully equipped with saloons, restaurants, hotels, "ladies of pleasure," and its fair share of gun-toting hoodlums.

For almost twenty years the miners burrowed into the mountainside, extracting over $40 mil-

CHURCH · RANDSBURG

lion of gold until by 1912 the area appeared to be exhausted and the fifty-three miles of tunnels were abandoned.

In 1914, Randsburg's second boom occurred. This time it was tungsten found at nearby Atolia. Because of the U.S.A. involvement in World War I, tungsten was an extremely valuable mineral and the get-rich-quick spirit brought miners pouring back into the town.

The ending of the war and the inevitable decline in the need for tungsten was offset by Randsburg's third and final boom—this time in silver. The Kelly Mine at Red Mountain produced over $20 million in ores until it too was exhausted in 1947.

Today the mountain region around Randsburg and Johannesburg is littered with the debris from the three boom periods. The town itself is a sleepy community. Paint peels off the old false front stores and those notorious dust-laden winds, the Mojave Zephyrs, frequently scream and whip through the empty streets. But Randsburg is not altogether lifeless. Many of its citizens are merely relaxing in preparation for the next boom.

RAND MARKET • RANDSBURG

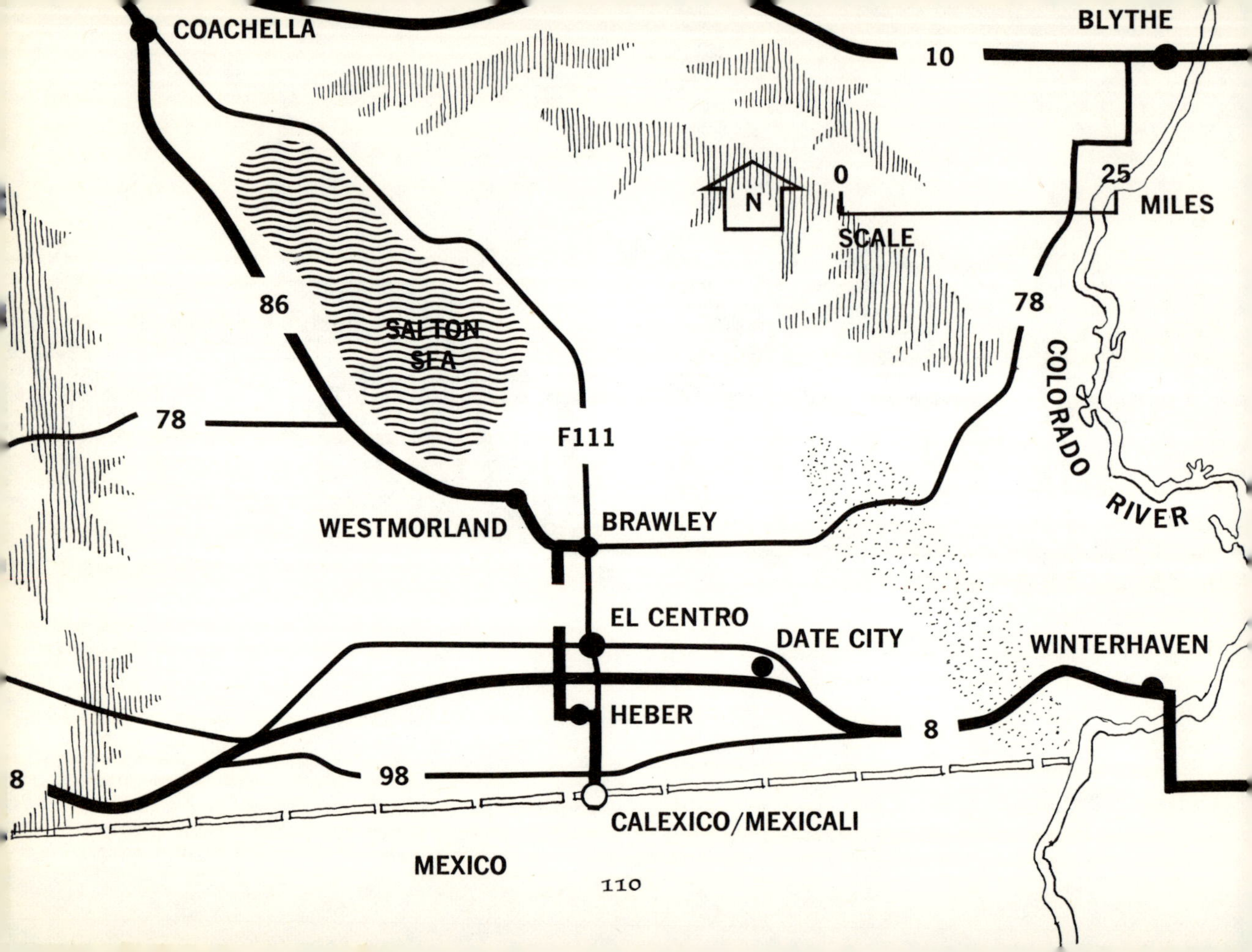

COACHELLA
BLYTHE
10
25
MILES
0
N
SCALE
86
78
SALTON SEA
78
COLORADO RIVER
F111
WESTMORLAND
BRAWLEY
EL CENTRO
DATE CITY
WINTERHAVEN
HEBER
8
98
8
CALEXICO/MEXICALI
MEXICO

The Imperial Valley

Immediately south of the Salton Sea lies a wide, flat belt of land which forms a substantial part of Imperial County. Prior to 1900 this land was a barren waste, subject to fierce sandstorms and occasional major floods from the Colorado River to the east. Today it is one of the richest agricultural areas in the world, renowned for the quality of its crops and livestock.

Its development, at least during the early stages, was due largely to the California Development Company which undertook a vast irrigation project in the valley in 1901. The mighty Colorado—otherwise known as the "Yellow Dragon" or more generously, the "Nile of America"—was the primary source of water supply.

That powerful river was a reluctant donor, and not until the floods of 1906 and 1907 had once again poured into the Salton Sea, was the Colorado finally tamed and the valley's future ensured. By 1910 over 250,000 acres had been converted from arid desert to fertile land. The introduction of the Southern Pacific and San Diego and Arizona Eastern rail lines across the valley encouraged the area's growth and the development of the major cities of El Centro, Imperial, Holtville and Calipatria.

Initially the valley attracted a wide cross-section of settlers, including a group of sturdy Swiss farmers, who established a substantial dairy industry. Today, most of the cities, particularly in the southern part of the valley, contain a large number of Mexican-Americans.

For the hunter of small town "gems" the valley cannot compare with other more historical parts of the State. These are working towns—the people of the valley were more concerned with making a new life than building architectural monuments to themselves. Nevertheless, some of the towns have charm, and one in particular, Heber, has a fascinating little history.

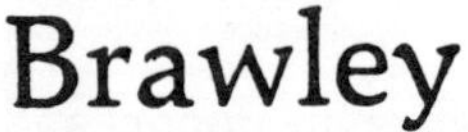

Brawley

SUN-CITY

Brawley, located at the junction of three major highways, is an example of one of the Imperial Valley's more successful towns. It acts as the agricultural marketing and service center for the northern sector and is famous for its Cattle Call

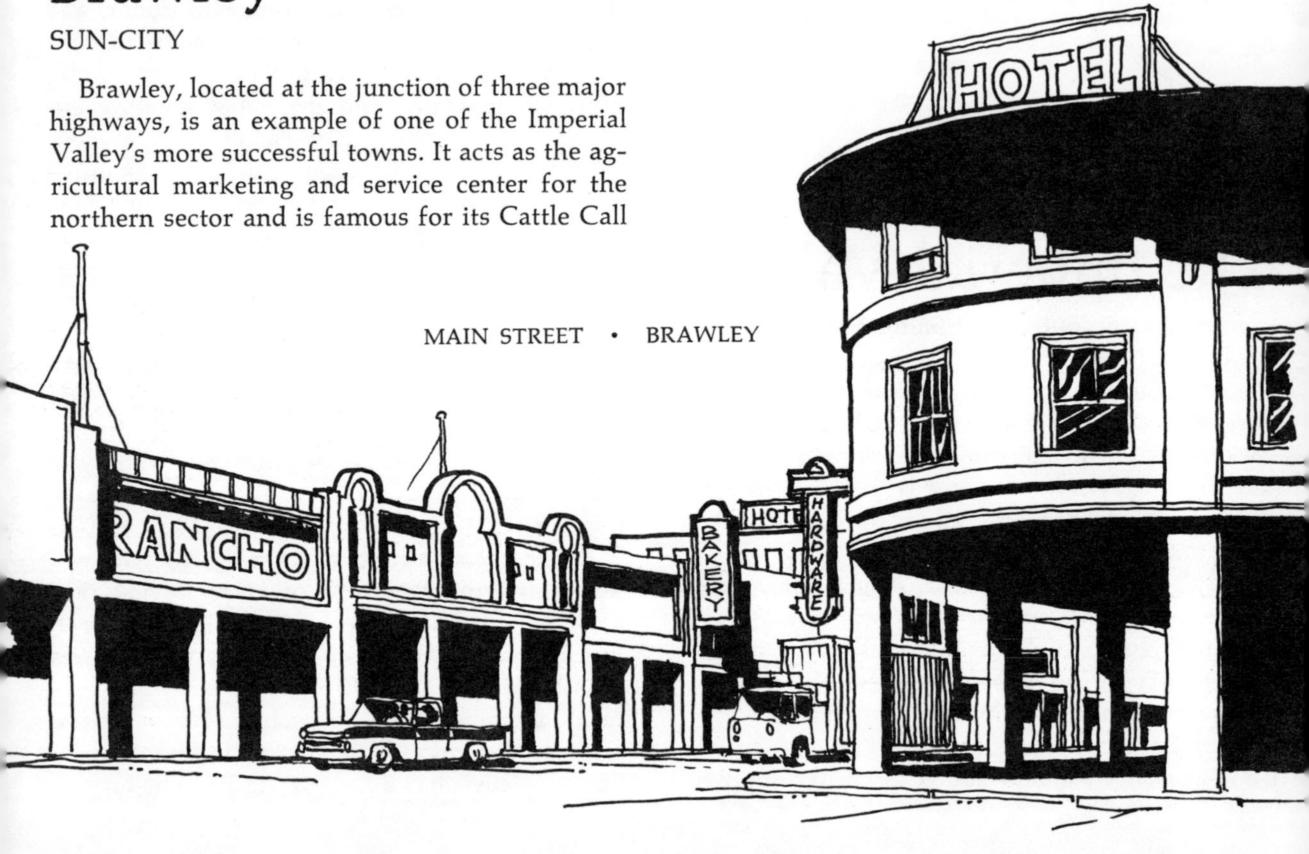

MAIN STREET • BRAWLEY

'Ball of Yarn'
FOR SALE
REALTOR

MOORISH-STYLED OFFICES • BRAWLEY

Rodeo and western celebration in November of each year.

In the torrid summer months the town swelters in a Saharan heat. The arcaded main street, matched in its uniformity only by downtown El Centro, provides a modicum of relief from the sun. Standing in its cool shadows in the mid-afternoon, the town seems lifeless except for the dull throbbing of overworked air conditioners.

A large part of Brawley was reduced to rubble in a 1940's earthquake. However, the Moorish-styled office of the irrigation district, just off main street, survived and is one of the most attractive architectural anomalies of the town.

Close to the Spanish-styled Civic Center at the west end of town is this ticky-tacky Los Angeles-style yarn store—an unusual pop-art feature in this solid no-nonsense town. Next door is a drive-in barber shop!

DATE CITY

Date City

A CITY THAT NEVER EXISTED

Place names are often misleading. The grandiose title of Date City refers in fact to a long low building with an undulating roofline which sits, or more precisely, languishes, by the roadside. It is all things to all people—a general store, bar, diner, trailer park, gas station and milestone. In all directions stretch the neatly cultivated fields of the valley. There are no other buildings at Date City—and, by the look of it, there never will be.

Heber

A SAD SAGA

The dust blows down the wide quiet streets of Heber and during the summer months, the scorching sun burns the flaking paint and cracked stucco of the town's few remaining buildings. It's hard to believe that a little over 60 years ago, the town was laid out in grandiose fashion as a major center for the Imperial Valley, complete with 100 feet wide tree-lined boulevards and its own agricultural college—the Heber Collegiate Institute, built in 1908. Today the porticoed college, with its 14 feet high rooms, sits in a tumbleweed field and slowly disintegrates.

A. H. Heber, who in conjunction with the Calexico Congregational Church, financed the agricultural campus, was a land developer of some renown when he was made president of the California Development Corporation in 1902. The Corporation was responsible for much of the early development in the valley and although it later fell into disrepute for failing to maintain a regular supply of irrigation water from the Colorado, Heber himself was always well regarded by the settlers.

Originally, the town of Heber was called Paringa. Its location at the proposed junction of the Southern Pacific and San Diego and Arizona Eastern railroads was expected to provide abundant impetus for growth. However, in those days, railroad alignments were determined less by logic and more by *bonuses* offered to the railroad companies by competing cities. Paringa

AGRICULTURAL COLLEGE • HEBER

KENNEDY'S MARKET • HEBER

PLOUGH · NEAR HEBER

somehow lost and El Centro, now a large flourishing city, became the junction point.

Heber's death, in a 1912 Los Angeles hotel fire, left the agricultural institute without financial backing. The town was shifted westward to a new location and the college was left abandoned in its empty campus. Growth was never significant. Abandoned farm machinery in nearby fields and the proud but almost deserted Kennedy Market tell of a dream which never materialized.

Westmorland

BOY'S TOWN

West Fifth Street, in the straggling, dusty town of Westmorland, was often referred to in more familiar terms as Boy's Town or Bordello Alley. The street, which is now totally sealed off, used to contain a score or so of cafes with names ranging from the standard Mom's Place, Joe's Place and Mexican Cafe to the more exotic

'CRIBS'   •   WESTMORLAND

Rumpus Room, Blue Bird, and My Blue Heaven.

Business flourished, particularly during the World War II era, when large military bases were established nearby. The street was a wide-open place known throughout the whole valley for the profusion of its poker games and the quality of its women. Then abruptly, on a hot afternoon in 1951, the street was sealed off. In one fell swoop, 263 ladies of pleasure were escorted from their tiny cribs at the rear of the cafes and were never seen again in the town.

Today the streeet is still intact. Empty glass bottles sit on dusty bars and the cramped cribs with their frame beds, sinks, pink walls and eloquent graffiti still remain as mementos of wild nights, long gone.

'BOYS TOWN' • WESTMORLAND

OLD STAGE COACH

Winterhaven

THE AMERICAN SAHARA

Winterhaven is a dusty straggling community located close to the Arizona border. The town's only redeeming feature is this unusual and fascinating bar which is surrounded by a melange of rusty machines including an old Model "T," fire engines, stagecoaches and wind-worn buggies.

The area surrounding Winterhaven however is rich in folklore and history. To the north around Glamis are the remains of countless gold-mines and the virtually non-existent town of Tumco once boasted the world's largest stamp mill which processed millions of dollars worth of ores extracted from the adjacent Cargo Muchacho Mountains.

To the east, almost directly on the Arizona border, is the Fort Yuma Military Post which was established in 1850 on a prominent bluff above the turbulent Colorado River. The St. Thomas

RED'S PLACE • WINTERHAVEN

Indian Mission, located within the compound, was built as a center for the conversion of the normally docile Yuman Indians whose only claim to notoriety was their massacre of the unfortunate Father Garces in 1781. Today the Indians live quietly in the nearby Yuman Reservation which is governed by its own tribal council.

The American Sahara located west of Winterhaven is a strange forty-mile long stretch of golden sand dunes, large parts of which are currently subjected to the ravages of dune buggies and similar off-road recreational vehicles. During World War II General Patton's tank corp trained here for the North African campaign against the Nazi hero, General Rommell. At one time the dunes were also a favorite location spot for Hollywood producers and scenes from *Beau Geste, Flight of the Phoenix* and many other desert-type classics were shot here.

Paralleling Route 8 as it passes through the dunes are remains of the "old plank road" built as a link between Yuma and the Imperial Valley and used by the tin-lizzies of the 20's. This old Mack truck never made it!

OLD MACK TRUCK

$2.95 EACH—WESTERN TRAVEL BOOKS FROM WARD RITCHIE PRESS

Trips for the Day, Weekend or Longer

ALL BOOKS COMPLETE, MANY WITH PHOTOGRAPHS AND MAPS

Quantity		TOTAL
☐	**Backyard Treasure Hunting**	$ _______
☐	**Baja California:** Vanished Missions, Lost Treasures, Strange Stories True and Tall.	$ _______
☐	**Bicycle Touring in Los Angeles**	$ _______
☐	**Book of the Road**	$ _______
☐	**Eat:** A Toothsome Tour of Los Angeles' Specialty Restaurants	$ _______
☐	**Exploring Big Sur, Monterey and Carmel**	$ _______
☐	**Exploring California Byways, #2** In and Around Los Angeles	$ _______
☐	**Exploring California Byways, #3** Desert Country	$ _______
☐	**Exploring California Byways, #4** Mountain Country	$ _______
☐	**Exploring California Byways, #5** Historic Sites of California	$ _______
☐	**Exploring California Byways, #6** Owens Valley, Inyo and Mono Counties	$ _______
☐	**Exploring California Byways, #7** An Historical Sketchbook	$ _______
☐	**Exploring California Folklore**	$ _______
☐	**Exploring the Ghost Town Desert**	$ _______
☐	**Exploring Historic California**	$ _______
☐	**Exploring the Mother Lode Country**	$ _______
☐	**Exploring Small Towns, No. 1:** Southern California	$ _______
☐	**Exploring Small Towns, No. 2:** Northern California	$ _______
☐	**Exploring the Unspoiled West, Vol. I**	$ _______
☐	**Exploring the Unspoiled West, Vol. II**	$ _______
☐	**Feet First:** Cityside and Countryside Walking Tours in Los Angeles	$ _______
☐	**Great Bike Tours in Northern California**	$ _______
☐	**Guidebook to the Canyonlands Country**	$ _______
☐	**Guidebook to the Colorado Desert of California**	$ _______
☐	**Guidebook to the Feather River Country**	$ _______
☐	**Guidebook to the Lake Tahoe Country, Vol. I.** Echo Summit, Squaw Valley & the California Shore	$ _______
☐	**Guidebook to the Lake Tahoe Country, Vol. II.** Alpine County, Donner-Truckee, & Nevada Shore	$ _______
☐	**Guidebook to Las Vegas**	$ _______
☐	**Guidebook to Lost Western Treasure**	$ _______
☐	**Guidebook to the Missions of California**	$ _______
☐	**Guidebook to the Mountains of San Diego and Orange Counties**	$ _______

☐ Guidebook to the Northern California Coast, Vol. I.
 Highway 1. $______
☐ Guidebook to the Northern California Coast, Vol. II.
 Humboldt and Del Norte Counties $______
☐ Guidebook to Puget Sound $______
☐ Guidebook to Rural California $______
☐ Guidebook to the Sacramento Delta Country $______
☐ Guidebook to the San Bernardino Mountains of
 California: Including Lake Arrowhead & Big Bear $______
☐ Guidebook to the San Gabriel Mountains of California $______
☐ Guidebook to Vancouver Island $______
☐ Hiking Maui: The Valley Isle $______
☐ Hiking the Santa Barbara Backcountry $______
☐ Meals on the Road $______
☐ Sabretooth Cats and Imperial Mammoths $______
☐ Saltwater Fishing in Southern California $______
☐ Ski Los Angeles $______
☐ Trees of the West: Identified at a Glance $______
☐ Where to Take Your Children in Nevada $______
☐ Where to Take Your Children in Northern California $______
☐ Where to Take Your Children in Southern California $______
☐ Where to Take Your Guests in Southern California $______

OTHER FINE GUIDEBOOKS

☐ Festivals of the West ($3.95) $______
☐ Guidebook to the Spas of Northern California ($1.95) $______
☐ Sierra Whitewater ($5.95) $______
☐ Walking Tours of San Juan Bautista ($1.95) $______
☐ Where to Find Gold in Southern California ($4.95) $______

WARD RITCHIE PRESS
474 South Arroyo Parkway
Pasadena, Calif. 90049

Please send me the Western Travel Books I have checked. I am enclosing $________ (check or money order). Please include 25¢ per copy to cover mailing costs. California residents add state sales tax.

Name ____

Address ____

City________________ State________________ Zip________